Praise for *The Marriage God Wants for You*

"A great resource on Christian marriage, at a time when we need to rejoice in the enduring grace of this wonderful sacrament. Cardinal Wuerl writes clearly and refreshingly on the call and vocation of married life. Bravo!"
—**Cardinal Timothy Dolan,** Archbishop of New York

"With his customary lucidity and depth, Cardinal Wuerl brings out the essential features of marriage as the Catholic Church understands it: fidelity, permanence, openness to life, and sacramentality. The book also includes some wonderful, funny, and gritty reflections from married couples themselves. I would warmly recommend it to anyone curious to know why the Catholic Church takes marriage with such seriousness and treats it with such reverence."
–**Fr. Robert Barron,** Rector, Mundelein Seminary, and founder, *Word on Fire* Catholic Ministries

"We live in a society that has emptied marriage of its glory—and stolen happiness away from families. Cardinal Wuerl restores that glory for young couples today. This book is an investment that will pay off in a happier future. Highly recommended!"
—**Scott Hahn,** bestselling author and professor of theology, Franciscan University of Steubenville

"Give your marriage this book as a gift! It is at once deeply profound and richly practical."
—**Matthew Kelly**, founder of DynamicCatholic.com and author of *Rediscover Catholicism*

"*The Marriage God Wants for You* is a mosaic of teaching, witnessing, recounting experiences, and sharing—a very fine 'workbook' for appreciating the structure, meaning, and beauty of marriage."
—**Cardinal Daniel DiNardo**, Archbishop of Galveston-Houston

"Cardinal Wuerl's refreshing re-presentation of marriage as high vocation, as sacrament, and as a vital social institution could not come at a better time. *The Marriage God Wants for You* will provide hope and encouragement to all who have embraced, or who are contemplating, a way of life that has become increasingly countercultural."
—**Mary Ann Glendon**, Learned Hand Professor of Law, Harvard University

"This is a book for people at every stage of the great adventure called marriage. Engaged couples, newlyweds, and those married for many years will all find enlightenment and encouragement in this clear and often eloquent exposition of the Christian meaning of matrimony. An added bonus are the moving testimonies of people who have lived it themselves."
—**Russell Shaw**, journalist and author

"*The Marriage God Wants for You* is a book for husbands and wives—and for husbands and wives-to-be—about how to ensure that your marriage will be the kind of union that a truly loving God, who supremely wills our fulfillment and happiness, wants us to have."

—**Robert P. George,** McCormick Professor of Jurisprudence, Princeton University

"What is the marriage God wants for you? One that reveals divine life to the world. Cardinal Wuerl clears up the confusion surrounding marriage today by using his well-known gifts of teaching and pastoring to describe the meaning and beauty of this sacrament."

—**Raymond Arroyo,** EWTN host and author of *The Prayers and Personal Devotions of Mother Angelica*

"Today marriage and family life is in a crisis. Within this darkness, Cardinal Wuerl's book on marriage brings the light of God's truth and the radiance of the Church's wisdom. May many young people and young married couples experience and know the joy, peace, and love that he offers them in this marvelous little treatise on Christian marriage."

—**Thomas G. Weinandy, OFM Cap,** lecturer, Dominican House of Studies and Pontifical Gregorian University, Rome

"Cardinal Wuerl has penned a most optimistic book on the positive beauty of the Christian understanding of marriage, and the divine love it both symbolizes and strengthens sacramentally. It is about what is right, not only about what is wrong. A beautiful contribution!"
—**John Michael Talbot,** musician and founder, Brothers and Sisters of Charity

"*The Marriage God Wants for You* is a beautiful and practical meditation on the Sacrament of Marriage at a time of wholesale confusion and doubt. Cardinal Wuerl has given a great gift to the Church at a critical moment for our culture."
—**Matthew E. Bunson, PhD,** author and editor of *The Catholic Answer* and *The Catholic Almanac*

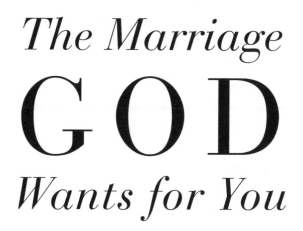

The Marriage GOD *Wants for You*

WHY THE SACRAMENT MAKES ALL THE DIFFERENCE

Cardinal Donald Wuerl

Archbishop of Washington

theWORD among us® press

Published by The Word Among Us Press
7115 Guilford Drive
Frederick, Maryland 21704

19 18 17 16 15 1 2 3 4 5

ISBN: 978-1-59325-280-9
eISBN: 978-1-59325-473-5

Cover design by Andrea Alvarez

Made and printed in the United States of America

Library of Congress Control Number: 2015940593

CONTENTS

FOREWORD

By Mike Aquilina

I had been watching my confessor's hairline inch farther and farther up his scalp—and suspected that I was the cause of it.

At the time, I was new to fatherhood—and still relatively new to marriage—and wondering why God hadn't included user manuals with all these strange and wondrous creatures he had sent to my home. Some days I felt as if I couldn't please any of them. And on some days they weren't pleasing me. Worse yet, I feared that none of this was pleasing to God.

Which was the reason I kept visiting my confessor again and again—until finally one day it dawned on me. That user manual I wanted—he was it! Whenever I went to see him, it seemed that I always came home with good advice—and a mission. And things at home always improved, even if only a little.

It was my confessor who helped me find more time to pray each day—without my losing a single minute from all my other tasks. It was the same confessor who eased me, without my noticing it, into the habit of asking whether *I* might be the source of this or that particular problem and not everyone else.

I liked the effect this was having on my inner life. But more than that, I liked the effect it was having on my home life, my marriage, and my parenting.

That confessor with the receding hairline was just the first of many confessors in my life. When he was moved to his next assignment, I just made myself part of his successor's schedule—and then the next guy's, and the guy after him. And I have never been disappointed.

Just how are these celibate men able to give such helpful advice about matters of marriage, from sharing chores to the mysteries of sex? I had to conclude that it was what they understood about the Sacrament of Matrimony.

That's what this book is all about. Marriage in Christ is a high calling, a vocation, but one in which the Lord pours out his grace on husband and wife so that they can truly become one flesh.

In *The Marriage God Wants for You*, Cardinal Wuerl, a priest and bishop who has a gift for teaching the faith, explains what a sacramental marriage is and is not. It is not just a feeling, but a decision to love. It is not just a contract, but a covenant. It is not a provisional arrangement that lasts as long as things are working well, but a lifelong union—one that is open to new life, the fruit of the love that is shared between husband and wife. Sacramental marriage is a vocation of love, and just like any vocation, it requires effort, discipline, and sacrifice.

In this book, Cardinal Wuerl draws on a rich spiritual tradition that is based on thousands of years of human experience. It is a tradition that is rooted in God's plan for us, his creation. And because the Lord knows us better than we know ourselves, the Church has an invaluable wealth of wisdom to offer about marriage. For example, studies have shown that couples who keep the Church's teachings on sexual morality are more than ten times as likely to stay married than couples who don't. Ten times!

But we need the grace of the sacraments—the grace of the Sacrament of Marriage as well as Confession and the Eucharist—to keep our sacramental marriage intact and thriving.

Which is why I keep going back to Confession. Marriage involves the most personal aspects of our lives—and the most delicately interpersonal. When we hit a snag in communications, when we come to disagreement on something important, a spouse (or both spouses) can feel very much alone, very vulnerable, and very exposed. Priests are trained in confidentiality—and bound by a seal of secrecy that's secured by the Church's most severe sanctions. From the many thousands of people they've counseled, they've seen problems from all sides—husbands, wives, children, in-laws. Priests have the goods, and they can be trusted. And when I exit the confessional, I receive not only good advice, but the grace to keep me going—even when the going gets tough.

I have been married for thirty years to my wife, Terri. We have six children. I count myself an immeasurably happy man. Sacramental marriage has brought God into our union, and that has given us the grace to endure and thrive. I am eternally grateful to those confessors who have helped me recognize that grace and draw from it.

I have known Cardinal Wuerl for much of my adult life, and I count him a dear friend. I do not hesitate to ask his advice when I'm in need. And when I ask, I know I shall receive. My family is better because he's in my life. My marriage is better because he's my friend.

So I owe much to the author of this book. I am so pleased that you, too, now have the opportunity to benefit from his advice. Use it well. It will make for a happier home, a happier life, and a happier world.

Mike Aquilina is the author of many books. He and his wife, Terri, have been married since 1985 and have six children.

PREFACE

This book bears my name on its cover, and I have written much of it. Some of it I wrote many years ago when I was helping to launch a curriculum called "The Catholic Vision of Love." Other portions were written more recently as I prepared for the Church's Synod on the Family. Everything inside, however, has been reshaped as I sought to fashion a single book.

As you'll see, however, I've had a lot of help. My friend Mike Aquilina contributed a foreword. Another friend, Helen M. Alvaré, penned a beautiful afterword. And in the spaces between the chapters, many other people—women and men who prefer to remain anonymous—have generously contributed their own perspectives and have drawn from their own experiences of married life. You'll find these at the end of each chapter under the heading "Bonds of Love." The book is so much richer for these voices. I thank them for their contributions, and I pray for them among my benefactors.

I pray for you, too, as you find yourself in the midst of a great adventure: as you begin, or continue, or dream about the marriage God wants for you.

Cardinal Donald Wuerl
Archbishop of Washington

A VOCATION TO LOVE

Over the years, the celebration of Valentine's Day has become a huge business for the greeting card, flower, candy, and jewelry industries. If you talk to people in love—whether young or old—you can sense a certain pressure on them to find the perfect gift. They want to find an item that sums up their love and expresses it perfectly.

But is there really a gift that can do such a thing? While many people may remember their favorite gift, you'll find very few who can recall every single Valentine's Day present.

It's my privilege as a bishop to celebrate significant anniversaries with couples who have enjoyed many years together. Every year, in every church I've served as bishop, we have observed a special day with a special Mass for couples marking a significant "jubilee"—a twenty-fifth, fiftieth, sixtieth, or even seventieth anniversary. We typically host this Jubilee Mass in a church that can accommodate a crowd—many couples with their many generations of offspring. It is a day of profound love made abundantly visible, a day of astonishing joy.

When I talk with these couples after Mass, I often ask them what they've learned through the years and what moments they remember most fondly. Sometimes people will mention a material gift—diamonds or roses—but usually only in passing.

I am struck by how many say that the gifts that mean the most are small gestures and quiet, ordinary acts done in love. I hear about the moment of discovery when one spouse suddenly realizes how much the other sacrifices each day. I hear about difficulties endured with a smile. I hear about one person secretly scrimping and saving so that another—or others in the family—can know a greater joy. I hear, again and again, about the quiet, constant giving of time, attention, consolation, and affection, all for the sake of that special someone else.

Rings and bouquets are beautiful, but they are not nearly as memorable as an action that rises spontaneously and decisively from the heart. What the jubilee couples have learned is that these moments represent the truest gifts. These gestures are the summary expressions of a love that cannot be contained by a box, wrapped up in paper, or tied with a bow.

Ordinary deeds of love will always exceed the value of anything that can be bought. Their value is not in the materials they're made of but rather in the far greater gift that they signify.

This book is all about that gift.

❖   ❖   ❖   ❖   ❖

The Bible tells us that we are made in the image and likeness of God (Genesis 1:26-27). The Bible also tells us that "God is love" (1 John 4:16). We are made, then, to resemble a God whose very identity is love.

15

We have been created from a divine blueprint, and so we all have a vocation to love. Our purpose in life is to love as God loves. Nothing less will fulfill us. Nothing less will make us happy.

God calls each of us to give ourselves totally in love, no matter what our circumstances may be. Love is a donation of one's entire life for the sake of another—and then for a wider circle of others. This is the vocation of priests and bishops and religious sisters and brothers. And it is the vocation of every married couple. In priesthood, in religious consecration, and in matrimony, God calls human beings—who are hardly equipped for the task—to a life of total self-giving. He calls us not just to give jewelry or greeting cards but, rather, to give of ourselves. If we do find ourselves giving anything else, then we should know that the gift we wrap is merely a symbol of something far greater. When we respond to God's call, we are giving our lives, which are in turn a reflection of God's infinite life and love.

This is the particular calling of married life. By the grace of the Sacrament of Matrimony, a couple's natural and mutual love is made infinitely stronger. It comes to share the strength and quality of God's eternal love. Something that is beautiful in its natural state—the marriage of a man and a woman—comes to shine with a supernatural radiance, with a light that never dims but rather grows brighter over the course of years.

Marriage, in its natural state, is a great creation of almighty God. But sacramental marriage is something still greater. It is a sharing in God's life—and a sharing of God's life with the world around us.

Marriage is a beautiful state of life. But marriage needs God's help, for men and women are hobbled by sin. We are born with a tendency to selfishness that we cannot overcome through merely human power. Only with God's grace can we overcome our common enemies, which Scripture and tradition identify as the world, the flesh, and the devil.

The good news is that God wants to give us the grace we need. If God has called us to a certain state of life, then he will give us everything we require to live faithful to his call. But he will not force his will upon us, and we do need to cultivate the habit of seeking his help. If we ask for it, we will receive it.

I fear, however, that many people have lost the habit of going to God for help. And as a result, marriages have suffered terribly. I do not need to demonstrate that this is so. This is not the place to cite statistics about divorce, infidelity, cohabitation, and the increasing aversion to commitment among young people. If you read the papers, watch television, or surf the Internet, you know as much as you need to know.

Yet you also know that there is, in men and women, young and old, an enduring dream of lasting love. There is an abiding admiration for couples who hold fast to one another through all manner of difficulties. Theirs are the stories that inspire. Theirs are the stories people flock to see in movies and read about in romantic novels. This popular appeal itself tells us something. It testifies to a deep-seated longing of the human heart and a hope for fulfillment in human love.

We are made for love, and Love made us that way.

❖   ❖   ❖   ❖   ❖

Love is a vocation, a calling, and so God's grace is necessary to sustain it.

Spouses, like clergy, are called to share God's holiness in a very specific way. Husbands and wives must build up the Church and even build "churches." It was a custom of the early Christians to call the home "the domestic church," because home is where the faith begins, and home is where it must grow.

You've probably heard the old saying "Charity begins at home." It's true, and it's a statement of tremendous consequence, because charity is the greatest love possible. Charity, from the Latin word *caritas*, is the very love that we identify with God.

Charity is love that reflects God's love for his people. It is love that flows from heaven to fill the earth. In the context of marriage and family life, charity is the channel of grace that moves each member of the family to be self-giving in service to the others. Such love is fruitful, so it is the gift that keeps on giving.

Pope Francis spoke about the vocation of marriage and the love experienced in the family, and he reminded us of how ordinary charity appears when we see and hear it in action.

In order to have a healthy family, three words need to be used. And I want to repeat these three words: please, thank you, sorry. Three essential words! We say please so as not to be forceful in family life: "May I please do this? Would you be happy if I did this?" We do this with a language that seeks agreement. We say thank you, thank you for love! But be honest with me, how many times do you say thank you to your wife, and you to your husband? How many days go by without uttering this word, thanks! And the last word: sorry. We all make mistakes, and on occasion someone gets offended in the marriage, in the family, and sometimes—I say—plates are smashed, harsh words are spoken, but please listen to my advice: don't ever let the sun set without reconciling. Peace is made each day in the family: "Please forgive me," and then you start over. Please, thank you, sorry![1]

By such simple acts of love, marriage and family are nourished and nurtured in a way that reflects the very life of the Church. Indeed, it is the life of the Church! It is a continuation of our Holy Communion, which makes us one in Jesus Christ. It is an extension of our experience of the grace of Confession and reconciliation. Unless God's charity pervades the ordinary life of Catholic families, the Church is failing at its task to spread the gospel.

As important as this task is, it requires no special programs or burdensome budgets. It requires small and simple acts of love.

❖ ❖ ❖ ❖ ❖

Even Catholics are prone to forget that Valentine's Day is named for a saint. February 14 is the feast of St. Valentine, a Christian of the third century who was loved throughout the city of Rome. We don't know much about St. Valentine's life. He lived a long time ago, during a century of harsh persecution when it was difficult to keep documentary records.

According to some old legends, Valentine was a priest who blessed marriages at a time when the pagan authorities were trying to prevent Christians from establishing families. Such measures were typical of the third-century persecutions, when Rome tried repeatedly to limit the Church's growth. If Christians were denied the right to marry, then they could not establish "domestic churches."

If Valentine continued to witness and bless Christian marriages, then he committed a countercultural act—an act of civil disobedience for the sake of the Christian family. If indeed he did that, then we could say that he earned his lasting association with love's big yearly holiday.

Unfortunately, we have no way of confirming those ancient stories, and all we know for sure about Valentine is that he died a martyr.

Even so, I think that's enough for us to know. If he died a martyr, then we know that he loved with his whole being. He gave his life, and he held nothing back. And that should be our common standard for every human love.

Two thousand years ago, St. Paul urged spouses to love one another "as Christ loved the church" (Ephesians 5:25). Well, how did Christ love the Church? He laid down his life for it (John 10:17-18). He did this not only at the moment of his death, but all through his life. He expressed divine love through many everyday acts of love—healing, forgiving, admonishing, encouraging, instructing, accompanying.

His whole life was a gift of love, given for others. He gave himself as the gift, and everything else was a sign, a symbol, an expression, and a mystery of his divine love.

So many of those signs he entrusted to his Church so that they would always be with us as expressions of love. We call them "sacraments," and the one that St. Paul called a "great sacrament" (cf. Ephesians 5:32) is marriage.

A married couple is a visible sign of God's self-giving. They signify God's lasting love for his people. They signify the cross of Jesus and his glory. They signify the long-awaited healing of Adam and Eve. They signify the very life of the Trinity in heaven.

A Catholic couple who is well instructed in the faith, even if they have no money to buy a gift, have all that they need to give each other the perfect Valentine's Day gift every year: a long life together.

Bonds of Love

"Whoever does not love a brother whom he has seen cannot love God whom he has not seen" (1 John 4:20). This Scripture verse speaks volumes to me, especially when that "brother" is my husband.

It's not that I don't love my husband—of course I do, with all my heart. But how do I show my love? For some reason—and maybe this is true of most married couples—we save our worst behavior for our spouses.

Studies have shown that one of the main predictors of whether a couple will stay together is whether they are kind to one another. How simple, and yet how difficult! Why is it so easy to let a harsh word fall from my lips or to fail to really listen when my husband is speaking to me?

Couples will have arguments—we're fallen human beings and we're always working to overcome our selfishness and to lay down our lives for each other. But I'm talking about the day-to-day interaction. I want it to be filled with kindness, tenderness, and affection. That's how

I'd want to treat Jesus, and though I often fail to recognize it, my husband is the face of Jesus to me.

And so every day when I examine my conscience, the first thing I do is ask myself, "How did I treat my husband today? Did I speak with kindness and respect? Did I make it a point to hug him and tell him that I love him?" Too often I wince when I realize how I have fallen short.

But I know that's what God is calling me to do, no matter how often I fail. And I know that if I ask, God will give me the grace to be silent when I'm tempted to lash out, or to be attentive when I'm more interested in what I'm reading on my phone, or to be patient when I want to interrupt him with my own ideas of how things should be done.

After I've repented, I once again ask the Lord to make me a good wife, a kind wife, a wife who not only loves her husband, but also demonstrates it daily. I have seen so many times in several decades of married life that God honors such prayers. And for that I am eternally grateful—because when I'm kind and loving to my husband, I am also kind and loving to my Lord.

❖ ❖ ❖ ❖ ❖

My husband and I are very different. I am an extroverted affirmation junkie who enjoys socializing and talking through conflicts immediately. He is a contented introvert who needs time alone and who waits for his emotions to cool before responding to a situation.

Variety is the spice of life, but differences can cause misunderstanding and conflict. For example, I feel lonely when my husband and I sit in a room together reading and don't talk. I feel distant from him when he doesn't want to do something social or spiritual as a couple. I can look at other couples from church and think, "Why can't you be like her husband?" These thoughts send me down a problematic road. And dumping such thoughts and the accompanying negative emotions on my husband at the end of a long day is a recipe for disaster.

In our marriage class, we've talked about spouses having a preferred way to receive love (also known as "love languages," as described by Christian counselor and author Gary Chapman). Ideally, each spouse should try to communicate love in the way most helpful to the other and try to recognize and receive the love being expressed by the other spouse.

I thought that God wanted me to pray to recognize and receive the love that my husband was giving me rather than focusing on what I wasn't getting. One Friday night, after struggling with loneliness all week, I repented of my grumbling and prayed to the Holy Spirit. I didn't have to wait long for an answer!

The next morning, while I was praying, my husband came down the stairs. When I jumped up and began to make coffee, he said to me, "Why can't you just let me be nice to you?" Then he began making breakfast. God began to open my eyes to see that he was loving me through acts of service: shoveling snow (again!), taking our resistant twelve-year-old son to the barber, and working on our tax returns.

As I experienced love from my husband, my heart began to soften and my critical views began to change. I was able to love him by contentedly sitting with him on the couch watching college basketball with popcorn. And the Holy Spirit surprised me again when my husband was able to make a breakthrough with one of our children, helping her to be reconciled with us and with her sister.

I know that my husband and I express our love in very different ways. But God can work through our differences, strengthening our marriage through the very things that could divide us. In the process, the Lord is expanding my own heart so that I might see and love my husband as he does. I am fortunate to be in a "bilingual" marriage!

CHAPTER 1

THEN COMES MARRIAGE

Weddings are joyful events, and so many of our customs are designed to convey that joy. The bride and groom dress up in perhaps the finest clothing they will ever wear. Their friends and family members travel great distances to spend a day in celebration. There is special music.

The marriage God wants for you begins with a wedding in a church. The wedding is joyful because it's a new beginning. But a wedding is just a beginning. A wedding has to become a marriage, and for that to happen, the bride and the groom need to have a clear understanding of what they've begun— what kind of commitment they've made.

For thousands of years, there was a strong common agreement about the nature of marriage. Marriage was the bond that held together not only households but all of society. It was the institution that enabled individuals, families, and communities to achieve a greater measure of security, happiness, and prosperity.

For society at large, the consensus about marriage has fallen apart in recent generations, leading to widespread insecurity, misery, and poverty—material, emotional, and spiritual. Powerful people in the media, government, and academia have rejected traditional marriage and even worked for its demise, but they have proposed nothing constructive or coherent to replace it. The experiment with "alternative" lifestyles is failing.

For Catholics, marriage remains today what it has always been. A couple who seek a Catholic wedding—and who understand and accept what that means—can truly enter into the joy of the Lord on their special day. They have something to celebrate. The glossary of the *Catechism of the Catholic Church* spells out a useful definition of marriage:

> A covenant or partnership of life between a man and woman, which is ordered to the well–being of the spouses and to the procreation and upbringing of children. When validly con-tracted between two baptized people, marriage is a sacrament.

That is the blueprint for a faithful and happy life.

Have you ever watched from the sidewalk as a high-rise building went up? You know that the apartments or offices on the top floor will be beautiful, but only because the architects put great care into drawing up the blueprints. Long before the first spade went into the earth, the builders knew what the finished building would look like. They knew what materials they would need. They knew the task that lay ahead. Ignor-ing the blueprints was never an option because small mistakes at any stage could endanger the entire project—the structure and everyone inside.

The marriage God wants for you is more important than any building that has ever been constructed. To you in particular, it is more important than any of the Seven Wonders of the World—but not only to you. It is supremely important to your parents and siblings, your neighbors and friends, and especially to the children you may have some day.

Your marriage is, moreover, a primary concern for the God who created you and who called you to share your life with a spouse. Your spouse represents your particular path to happiness and fulfillment. Body and soul, you were designed for your particular marriage. God made you for it. And that is the deepest reason so many people are joyful when they gather in the church for a wedding. They are witnessing God's plan as it unfolds. They are witnessing a couple saying yes to the life that God has planned for them since the beginning of creation.

God's blueprint makes possible the joy of completion, not only on the wedding day, but also through the highs and lows of ordinary married life. As the Good Book says, "Unless the LORD build the house, / they labor in vain who build" (Psalm 127:1).

The traditional blueprint for marriage has proven successful in producing good lives over the course of centuries and even millennia. No other lifestyle has presented a comparable alternative. Since this book is about building according to God's plan, let's spend this chapter looking closely at the terms of the definition.

Marriage is a covenant. The definition starts with a word that may seem strange or vague to us. But it is the word that the

Church, in recent years, has preferred for its description of marriage. The word is "covenant." As Pope St. John Paul II preached in one of his homilies, "In marriage, a man and a woman pledge themselves to each other in an unbreakable *covenant* of total mutual self-giving, and they promise to remain faithful to one another to the end, in spite of whatever difficulties may come."[2]

Sometimes, too, the Church will speak of a marriage "contract." In the same homily quoted above, St. John Paul said, "The marriage contract is an unconditional and enduring covenant."

So we see that the marriage bond is both a covenant and a contract. What's the distinction?

A contract is a formal, legally binding agreement that governs the exchange of goods or services. Since marriage is a union of two lives, it involves such an exchange. The couple will share their property. They will hold everything in common. Even their individual bodies will belong each to the other! They promise to love and honor one another and care for one another in sickness and health. Their vows are concerned with goods and services.

Surely, however, the terms we see in the marriage vows strain the limits of what a contract can bear. And so we say that they are more than a contract. They are a covenant.

A covenant, too, is formal and legally binding, but it is more than simply a contract between two human parties. It is a binding agreement that invokes almighty God, who alone can join two people and make them one. With the invocation of God, everything changes. The contract achieves the dignity of a covenant—and it may not be broken.

Once at a wedding, I heard the groom describe marriage as a three-party covenant: the groom and bride make a covenant with one another, and the two of them make their covenant with Christ.

Marriage is a partnership of life. Even in the secular world, contracts and covenants are commitments that bear consequences. The commitment of marriage is lifelong. The couple place no limits on their partnership. There is no expiration date. There is no possibility of reconsideration in a few years or in a few decades. What's more, it is a partnership that encompasses all of life. Each holds nothing back from the union. Whatever one has—possessions, time, affection—belongs entirely to the other.

Marriage is between a man and a woman. This is a basic truth of biblical religion, spelled out clearly in the opening chapter of the first book of our Scriptures, Genesis. It is, moreover, built into the fabric of creation. The two sexes, male and female, are complementary in body and mind. Each completes the other in the formation of a family. Until quite recently, no civilization in human history had ever honored anything as marriage except the union of a male and a female.

Marriage is ordered to the well-being of spouses. Spouses look out for one another and care for one another. They consult one another as they make important decisions. They pool their resources and save for a future they intend to share. For these reasons, and others, married people tend to live longer and enjoy better health than those who remain single. It is not good to be alone, and marriage ensures a certain constancy in companionship and care.

Marriage is ordered to the procreation and upbringing of children. But marriage is not just about one person's health or even the health of two people. Married love is expansive. It creates the conditions of greater generosity and still greater love. Marriage is an act of hope for the future. Marriage is the best environment in which to raise society's next generation. The union of a man and a woman naturally leads to the conception of children. This is the ordinary course of love in the world as God created it: spousal love leads to parental love, which further strengthens the love of the spouses.

Marriage is a sacrament. The Church recognizes many rituals, many human relationships, and many good works. Only a few, however, have been honored as sacraments since the beginning of Christianity. The seven sacraments are Baptism, Confirmation, Eucharist, Penance, the Anointing of the Sick, Holy Orders, and Matrimony. The sacraments are special signs that Jesus established and entrusted to the Church for the purpose of sharing God's grace. They are privileged events—the most important events of our lives. Faith teaches us that they are *efficacious* signs. They're not merely symbols. They don't just "stand for" something else. They bring about the very thing that they signify. In the course of this book, we will look closely at the great heavenly realities signified, and realized, by marriage.

❖ ❖ ❖ ❖ ❖

These are the constituent elements of the marriage God wants for you. Of course, marriage is more than these elements, just as you and I are more than the sum total of carbon, hydrogen, oxygen, and nitrogen. Marriage is more because of its nature as a covenant and its status as a sacrament.

As a covenant, marriage represents the most solemn kind of partnership anyone could enter. A covenant creates an unbreakable family bond between two previously unrelated parties. "Covenant" is the word the Bible uses to describe God's relationship with his people. At key moments in history, God made special covenants with Noah, Abraham, Moses, and David. "Covenant" is the word Jesus applied to the greatest gift he gave us: the Holy Eucharist, which he referred to as the "new covenant" in his blood (Luke 22:20).

As a sacrament, marriage is a revelation of God's life and goodness in the world. It is an institution he protects, blesses, and guarantees with his grace.

We invite Christ into a Christian marriage because we know that we cannot make our way through life without him. We certainly cannot succeed in the commitment, the covenant, the partnership of marriage if Christ isn't a part of it.

Bonds of Love

My wife and I recently embarked on a twenty-fifth anniversary trip to the island where we had honeymooned, and took an extra day to visit the city in which we were engaged and married. On our way back to the airport, we chatted with our taxi driver, a relatively new husband and the father of an infant. He asked us what our secret was to such a long-lasting marriage. "We're still newlyweds," my wife replied, expressing the need to keep things fresh and to actively love one another in spontaneous ways.

Just then, the memories of our many meetings with a parish priest at the church just down the road came flooding back to me. No, our marriage hasn't been perfect, and yes, we have had our struggles. But the priest who prepared us taught us well, and we have held firm to the understanding of the Church's teaching of marriage as a sacrament and covenant, a sign of Christ's love for his bride, the Church (Ephesians 5:25). In a loving, pastoral way, Father made sure we understood and accepted the holy magnitude of the vows we would make. But he also reassured us that our cooperation with God's grace would give us the strength to live out our covenant.

And so, after many meetings with the priest, our view of our future changed. We no longer thought of our upcoming marriage as a fairy-tale fling that would be sustained by warm and cozy feelings and the perfect attraction of our personalities. We realized that we were being called to love one another sacrificially, no matter what. "Till death do us part" does not mean "unless he becomes unattractive or paralyzed" or "unless she betrays me." Jesus loved all the way to the cross, and we must be prepared to do the same.

Our embrace of Church teaching from the beginning has truly sustained us in every trial. We strive for our love to be a reflection of Jesus' love to all we encounter. We don't live up to this ideal in every instance. But thanks to one parish priest who spent many hours with a young man and his fiancée, we have sustained this beautiful covenant of love for more than a quarter century.

❖　❖　❖　❖　❖

When my wife's mother died in the first few years of our marriage, my wife did not persist in her grief but decided to tend relationships with her siblings, her father, and extended family. Over the years, she has supported her sister, who suffers from mental illness, her father, who was afflicted with alcoholism and diabetes, and her brother, who struggled with advanced-stage liver cancer. I have always admired her love for her family.

But my own relationship with extended family members has been different. I brought the baggage of distant and strained relationships with parents and with half brothers and sisters into our marriage. So I usually ignored them.

All that changed when three of my older siblings became desperately ill within a handful of years. First, my brother Claude was diagnosed with leukemia. My temptation was to isolate myself from his suffering. My wife gently challenged me to call him once a week. I learned later that he had looked forward to our Sunday conversations all week long.

Within a year, my oldest brother, Andre, began to slip into advanced Alzheimer's. Again, my wife prodded me to visit him before his disease progressed any further. So I did. I asked him for forgiveness for the ways in which I had hurt him while we was growing up. Then I thanked him for sharing his conversion to Jesus and told him that his witness had led me to Christ.

Only months later, my oldest sister, Louise, was severely injured from a fall down a flight of stairs. My wife nudged me once again. We visited Louise, and I thanked her for the Bible she had given me after my First Communion. I also thanked her for her lifelong example of ministry in her parish. She had inspired me to take my first job working with the poor in the inner city.

All three of my siblings died within three years. I believe that God uses our spouse to speak to us, to call us on to holiness. It's part of his plan for marriage. I thank God for saving me from a life of regrets through my wife's patient encouragement. I thank God that he gave me the humility to hear his voice speaking through my wife, calling me into deeper communion with my own family.

CHAPTER 2

FOLLOW THE SIGNS

Circling the city where I live is a beltway that bears many lanes of traffic. Residents know the route very well, but visitors depend upon the road signs. Signs tell you how far you are from your exit. Signs tell you how fast you may drive. Signs warn you away from hazards. Signs estimate the travel time to common destinations. Some signs simply present symbolic images for a message that needs no words: the outline of a gas pump or a construction worker in a hard hat. Other signs offer simple, helpful advice: *slow down, stay alert, proceed with caution.*

If you're a stranger in a strange land, it's best to pay attention to the signs, even if you have a GPS. Otherwise, a sudden detour could leave you disoriented and lost.

We have already noted that Christian marriage is a sign. In this chapter we'll examine what that means.

A sign is an object that points beyond itself. It signifies something else, something greater than itself. The large green interstate sign that says "Baltimore" is not itself the city that goes by that name. The sign points the way to the city.

In the Gospels, the word "sign" is often used to describe a miracle or extraordinary event initiated by Jesus (Mark 16:20; Luke 21:25; John 2:11). The sign points to Jesus. It is a manifestation and a proof of his divine power.

Jesus established the sacraments to accomplish in the Church what his miracles had accomplished during his earthly ministry. In those days, he fed great multitudes with a few loaves and fishes; now, he feeds hundreds of millions with himself, with his Eucharistic Body and Blood. Then, he cured people of diseases that kept them from thriving; now, he heals the infirmity of sin, which would keep us from sharing eternal life. The miracles in the Gospels are signs that point forward to the sacraments of the Church. What Jesus did for blind beggars and grieving widows, what he did for the wedding party that had run out of wine, he now does for you and me in far more powerful ways. When he healed the paralytic in Capernaum, he even told the witnesses that the forgiveness of sins was a greater sign than the cure of the paralyzed man (Mark 2:9-11).

In a sense, everything in the world is a sign. Everything created tells us something about the Creator, just as every work of art tells us something about the artist. There are, however, no signs more important for us than the signs that we know as sacraments. These are signs of God's covenant with us. These are signs of God's saving power. And marriage is one of those few supremely important signs.

The *Catechism*'s glossary, again, provides a helpful definition, this time of the word "sacrament":

> An efficacious sign of grace, instituted by Christ and entrusted to the Church, by which divine life is dispensed to us through the work of the Holy Spirit.

A sacrament is an outward material sign or gesture. In Baptism, it involves water. In the Eucharist, it involves bread and wine. In marriage, it involves the bodies: the very lives of the husband and wife.

These signs, however, are different from anything in nature. They surpass nature—they are supernatural. In the natural order, signs point to something other than themselves, something more important than themselves. But sacraments are *efficacious* signs. They are the occasion of the thing they signify. The water of Baptism really bestows eternal life. The bread and wine of the Eucharist really become the Body and Blood of Jesus Christ. And the two who are joined in marriage, the husband and wife, really become one in Christ, and their unity is really unbreakable, lasting as long as their lives on earth.

Jesus set the sacraments in place. It was he who broke bread and said, "Do this in memory of me" (Luke 22:19). It was he who gave his apostles the power to forgive sins (John 20:23). It was he who commanded his disciples to baptize in the name of the Trinity (Matthew 28:19). And it was he who blessed marriage and elevated its significance when he performed his first miracle at a wedding reception in Cana (John 2:1-11).

It was St. Paul who referred to marriage as a sacrament. He used the Greek word *mysterion*, which is translated in Latin as *sacramentum*. In English we render these words as "mystery," or "sacrament." (Catholics in the Eastern churches use "mystery" to refer to the sacramental signs; Catholics in the West use "sacrament.") Thus, as St. Paul speaks of the one-flesh union, he says, "This is a great sacrament" or "This is a great mystery" (Ephesians 5:32).

Read the whole passage, and you'll see that he is talking about marriage as a sign that does more than simply signify. It becomes what it signifies. It is a new creation.

Be subordinate to one another out of reverence for Christ. Wives should be subordinate to their husbands as to the Lord. For the husband is head of his wife just as Christ is head of the church, he himself the savior of the body. As the church is subordinate to Christ, so wives should be subordinate to their husbands in everything. Husbands, love your wives, even as Christ loved the church and handed himself over for her to sanctify her, cleansing her by the bath of water with the word, that he might present to himself the church in splendor, without spot or wrinkle or any such thing, that she might be holy and without blemish. So [also] husbands should love their wives as their own bodies. He who loves his wife loves himself. For no one hates his own flesh but rather nourishes and cherishes it, even as Christ does the church, because we are members of his body.

> "For this reason a man shall leave [his] father
> and [his] mother / and be joined to his wife,
> / and the two shall become one flesh."

This is a great mystery, but I speak in reference to Christ and the church. In any case, each one of you should love his wife as himself, and the wife should respect her husband. (Ephesians 5:21-33)

Marriage, then, is an effective and lasting sign, just like Baptism. The unity of spouses is as enduring as God's communion with the Church. It is brought about not merely by their human wills but by an act of God, to which they give their full and free consent.

For Christians, marriage has great dignity because of the divine reality that it signifies. The sign is rich in significance. Sometimes readers boil it down to an equation: husband + wife = Christ + Church. But, as great as that equation is, the total significance of marriage is greater still.

Marriage signifies the union of Christ with the Church. The Church is one body, with Christ as its head. This is the great point of St. Paul's metaphor, which he elaborates not only in his Letter to the Ephesians but in other letters as well (see Romans 12:4-5; 1 Corinthians 12:12-27; Colossians 1:18). When Jesus appeared to Paul (then known as Saul) on the road to Damascus, the Lord made no distinction between himself and the members of his Church (see Acts 9:4-5). He *identified* with them so that anything done to them was done to him as well (see also Matthew 25:40). That's how close the union of Christ with the Church is—and that is the union that marriage signifies.

Marriage signifies the glory of heaven. In the Book of Revelation, St. John reports a vision of heaven, which he sees as a great wedding, the inseparable union of Christ with the Church. "I also saw the holy city, a new Jerusalem, coming down out of heaven from God, prepared as a bride adorned for her husband" (Revelation 21:2). A multitude of angels proclaim the great event:

> Let us rejoice and be glad and give him glory. / For the wedding day of the Lamb has come, / his bride has made herself ready. / . . . Blessed are those who have been called to the wedding feast of the Lamb. (Revelation 19:7, 9)

Marriage signifies the unity of the Blessed Trinity. Christians worship one God who is a communion of three Persons: the Father, the Son, and the Holy Spirit. We call this mystery the Trinity. The divine Persons are coeternal—none preceded any of the others. They are coequal—none is superior to any of the others in power or rank. They are united in an eternal bond of infinite love. The Persons of the Trinity can be distinguished, but never separated.

Marriage mirrors this by joining two spouses whose love is open to the presence of a third: a child. Saints from John Chrysostom of the fourth century to St. John Paul II of the twentieth century have seen the family's unity as a human image of divine love. Just as the Persons of the Trinity are not diminished by their mutual love, so the human person naturally flourishes in a loving family. The individual thrives in loving relationship with others.

Christian marriage signifies the healing of the human family. God created marriage and declared it "very good" (Genesis 1:31). Nonetheless, he created human beings with free will, and the first couple abused their freedom. Marriage was the context for humanity's original sin. Though husband and wife were created for the sake of helping one another (see Genesis 2:18, 20), they failed in this task, and together they gave in to the temptation to sin. From that moment on, life in human families was troubled by division, envy, resentment, infidelity, and dishonesty. The fault of the first couple has had consequences in every generation since the beginning.

Jesus appeared in history to save humanity from sin and its disastrous effects, especially on the family. So Jesus himself arrived by way of a family—Mary and Joseph of Nazareth. He inaugurated his public ministry at a wedding feast, and there he raised marriage to the dignity of a sacrament. If sin had until then been passed down through the human family, Jesus came to heal the problem at its root.

Christian marriage, then, is a sign that points to highest heaven. But it does far more than signify. As a sacrament, it brings about what it signifies. And so it gives two spouses, a husband and a wife, the divine power to make earthly life more heavenly. It gives them a share of the life of the Trinity—the life that is defined as love—and empowers them to share it with one another and with their children.

Marriage is a sign with extraordinary value and immense power. The road sign that shows the way to Baltimore has no real contact with Baltimore. That vast piece of metal has almost certainly never been to the Inner Harbor or Camden Yards.

Sacraments, however, are signs that share the life of the heavenly city they signify. And that's something the Church celebrates at every wedding and in every Christian marriage.

Every married couple is a proclamation of the gospel—a sign that can be seen by neighbors and friends.

Every married couple is a living sermon.

Every married couple is a window into heaven.

Every married couple is called to live up to the gift they've been given, to become the living sign that God has re-created them to be.

Bonds of Love

After sixteen years of marriage, my husband quietly announced to me, "I've been thinking about joining the Catholic Church." I quickly got him in contact with a priest, and to my great surprise, he enthusiastically embraced the teachings of the Church.

This was a blessed time for us as we both invited God's presence into our lives. We had experienced several turbulent years in the early part of our marriage, but things began to stabilize for us as a couple when we became more serious about our devotion to the Lord. First, we started saying grace at meals. Then, we got in the habit of daily prayer—even praying together at our front door before we began our arduous commutes to work each morning. Meanwhile, my newly converted spouse discovered Eucharistic adoration, a practice he introduced to me, a cradle Catholic!

As it turned out, going to adoration together proved to be a real gift from God. It gave us the strength to get through a nightmare that would unfold just a few years later. One day we received a call informing us that my husband's elderly father had been brutally murdered in a home-invasion robbery.

Thankfully, by this time we had developed a more prayerful, trusting relationship with our Lord. Going to adoration as a couple and praying on a daily basis gave us the strength to get through the grief, anger, and resentment that are experienced by families who are victims of violent crime. During adoration we both prayed that somehow we could be healed of our bitterness and anguish, and I asked God to help us forgive the person who had committed this crime so that we could move on with our lives.

We attended a support group designed for such families and, to our sorrow, saw several marriages dissolve within that group. In fact, I was concerned that our earlier marital problems might resurface and weaken our marriage as well. But as our prayer life intensified, our marriage just got stronger!

As we prepare to celebrate our forty-second wedding anniversary, we look back at that time with gratitude. We both believe that the grace we received through Eucharistic adoration and our daily prayer life gave us the strength as a couple to survive that horrible ordeal. We turned to the Lord and he brought us to a genuine place of healing and peace, with more spiritual strength than we had ever dreamed possible.

❖ ❖ ❖ ❖ ❖

We were expecting our third child. Our two children were beyond excited to have another new sibling, and at the sonogram, when my wife was twenty weeks along, we discovered that we were having a daughter. We named her Monica.

Two weeks later our joy was utterly shattered.

I was at work, near the end of my shift. My wife called my desk phone, but I was in a meeting and was not able to answer. Then my cell phone rang, then came a text and another call. My wife told me she was bleeding and cramping—terrible signs in any pregnancy.

Once we arrived at the hospital, the nurses quickly got my wife hooked up to several different machines. For five minutes, the technician searched, trying to find a trace of a heartbeat. "Don't worry," she said. "We'll get the doctor in here, and he'll be able to find it."

The doctor came in. No movement. No heartbeat.

The most horrific thing a parent can endure came to pass. Death had reached out its ugly hand and snatched our daughter from us. The weight of this realization was too much for us. "Is there anything I can do?" the technician asked.

"Is there a priest on staff?"

"I'll call for him."

Fr. Doug came within the hour. He prayed with us and blessed us. Much to my amazement, he also brought us the Eucharist. Christ did not just send his priest to console us. Just as he wept at the death of his dear friend Lazarus, Christ came himself and wept with us.

Once we came home, the love and support of our friends came pouring in. People brought us dinners and sent us money. They bought us memorial trees and prayed for us.

Friends of mine who are dear to me called me and told me similar stories of loss and grief. We were not alone—never alone! Our friends were with us; our family was with us; Our Lady and our God were with us.

The death of a child can easily unravel a marriage. But this was a time when Christ drew us closer. Without the sacramental grace of marriage, this would not have been something that either of us could have endured. God did not just make his presence known—he did not just help us through a difficult time. Through the sacramental grace of marriage, through the presence and assistance of his holy priests, through the help and outreach of our friends, he shouted his presence and screamed his love and sorrow for us at the loss of our beloved daughter.

CHAPTER 3

A LOVE THAT IS LIFELONG

We honor Augustine of Hippo as one of the great saints of the Church. Aside from the biblical authors, he is the writer most often cited in the *Catechism of the Catholic Church*. It was he who laid theological foundations for the Church's doctrine of marriage, and it was he who gave moral thinkers a vocabulary for the discussion of sexual ethics.

I'm pretty sure that all of these achievements would have surprised the neighbors and friends of the young Augustine. Though brilliant even in his adolescence, he was prideful and inclined toward trouble. His mother had raised him to be a Christian, but his pride and appetites led him to reject the life of faith.

He was sexually promiscuous for a time, and when he finally settled down with one woman in his young adulthood, they didn't bother to get married. They had a child out of wedlock, and they lived together for two decades, raising their child to adulthood before they finally parted ways.

Augustine eventually repented, converted to his childhood faith, and became a bishop. He wrote on many topics, from the Trinity to the proper ordering of society, but his writings on marriage and family are especially profound. Perhaps he understood the value of marriage so well because he had sinned against it so grievously in so many ways and for so many years. He knew the heartaches and heartbreaks he himself had caused. He saw the effects of his sins on his companion, his child, his mother, and his friends. He regretted the scandal he had caused, which had led others astray.

Writing in a psychologically and morally astute way, Augustine spoke often and beautifully of the "goods" of marriage. Perhaps that's because he had failed to understand them in his youth—and he had personally experienced the consequences of rejecting those goods.

He said that marriage is good because of three basic values: *fidelity*, *permanence*, and *the potential for offspring*. The convergence of these three goods is what distinguishes marriage from any other human relationship. And each of those three depends upon the others. If one element is missing, the others inevitably falter.

The marriage bond is faithful, and by that we mean monogamous and exclusive. A husband's affections and attention belong to his wife, and a wife's to her husband. From the earliest days of Christianity, sins of infidelity have been counted among the gravest offenses.

The marriage bond is permanent. It is unbreakable, secured by God. Separation cannot end it. Divorce cannot dissolve it. It is not dependent on feelings or desires. It is a commitment, a lifelong covenant, a new creation intended to endure.

Marriage is open to new life. Male and female are attracted to one another by nature, and the natural purpose of their attraction is the procreation of offspring. Human love grows from that simple fact of human nature. Men and women are fulfilled, not simply in drawing together, but rather in seeing their love extended to the next generation and beyond. Children help their parents to grow in many virtues, large and small: patience, generosity, unselfishness, industry, and frugality, to name just a few. As spouses draw together in loving their children, they become more lovable to one another.

Faithfulness. Permanence. Fruitfulness. These qualities are essential to marriage. Without all three of them, marriage loses its coherence. Without all three, the sign fails to signify what it should. It does not reflect the life of God, who is perfectly faithful, whose love is everlasting, and whose creation is abundantly fruitful.

❖ ❖ ❖ ❖ ❖

How do you tell a church from a supermarket? How do you tell a parking garage from a family home? Different structures have different characteristics—distinctive features that serve their particular purposes. The building is designed to accommodate the activities that will take place inside. That's why a gas station won't look like a church, and a church won't look like a supermarket. They have different functions, and so they have different designs.

So it is with marriage. We can identify a true marriage, not just the coming together of two people. We can identify a true marriage by those qualities, those goods, that we learned from St. Augustine—and that St. Augustine learned from Scripture. For Jesus was clear and uncompromising when he spoke of the permanent quality of the marriage covenant:

> Some Pharisees approached him, and tested him, saying, "Is it lawful for a man to divorce his wife for any cause whatever?" He said in reply, "Have you not read that from the beginning the Creator 'made them male and female' and said, 'For this reason a man shall leave his father and mother and be joined to his wife, and the two shall become one flesh'? So they are no longer two, but one flesh. Therefore, what God has joined together, no human being must separate." (Matthew 19:3-6)

The Pharisees pressed Jesus on the question, asking why he forbade divorce when Moses had permitted it.

Jesus responded that Moses had granted divorce as a concession to the weakness of his people. Divorce was not part of the original plan established in Genesis. It was not part of the original law given by God on Mount Sinai. It appears only later in the Book of Deuteronomy, the "second law" given by Moses on the plains of Moab after the Israelites' initial failures to keep God's law. Divorce was allowed, Jesus explained, "because of the hardness of your hearts" (Matthew 19:8). Then he declared a second marriage after divorce to be "adultery," unless the original marriage had been unlawful (19:9).

Even in the Old Testament, however—even when there was a legal concession for divorce—God made it clear through the prophets that the practice was to be abhorred. "For I hate divorce, / says the LORD, the God of Israel. . . . / You must not break faith" (Malachi 2:16).

Jesus' strong statements made clear that marriage need no longer be subject to its former weakened status. His saving action would restore marriage to its original dignity—and then raise it still further to be a sacrament of his new covenant.

In addressing the Pharisees' question, Jesus established a new, or rather renewed, norm for the faithfulness and permanence of marriage.

It is significant that he concludes his dialogue with an exhortation about openness to children: "Let the children come to me, and do not prevent them; for the kingdom of heaven belongs to such as these" (Matthew 19:14). Couples who live by Jesus' clear instructions are bringing about the kingdom.

❖ ❖ ❖ ❖ ❖

The design of marriage is evident in the vows taken by the husband and wife on their wedding day. The vows ensure that both spouses are committed to pursuing the goods God has built into marriage.

The commitment to permanence is everywhere. The priest or deacon asks, "Will you honor each other as man and wife for the rest of your lives?" And the couple answer, "I will" or "Yes." The vows that follow may take one of two forms, and both options emphasize that the commitment is binding for the course of a lifetime.

> I, (name), take you, (name), to be my wife/husband. I promise to be true to you in good times and in bad, in sickness and in health. *I will love you and honor you all the days of my life* (emphasis added).

> I, (name), take you, (name), for my lawful wife/husband, to have and to hold, from this day forward, for better, for worse, for richer, for poorer, in sickness and in health, *until death do us part* (emphasis added).

The vows may also be presented as questions, to which the bride and groom answer, "I do." But in every case, they are making an unqualified commitment to a permanent relationship, based not on circumstances or passions, but on God's grace.

It's easy to stay together in good times. If that were the extent of the commitment, it would hardly need a vow. The bad times present the challenge, and they're the reason for the vow.

Yes, husbands and wives are promising something humanly impossible. Yes, they're acting without full knowledge of what the future will hold. But nothing is impossible with God (Luke 1:37). God honors the vows of husband and wife and gives them the grace they need to get through difficult times—sickness and poverty and far worse. If they call upon the grace of the sacrament, they will pull through, and they will emerge stronger.

Nor is the good of fruitfulness neglected in the marriage ceremony. Near the beginning of the "Statement of Intentions," the priest or deacon asks the couple, "Will you accept children lovingly from God and bring them up according to the law of Christ and his Church?" To which they respond, "I will" or "Yes."

The terms of the covenant are as clear in the marriage vows as they are in Jesus' teaching—as they are in the fabric of God's creation in its original goodness.

❖ ❖ ❖ ❖ ❖

When you and I were children, so many of the stories we read ended with the words "And they lived happily ever after." As we grew up, however, we came to realize that not every story ends "happily ever after." And that's true of some marriages.

Today, sad to say, we are confronted with a rather large number of failed, broken, and nonfunctioning marriages. We look to the gospel vision at one horizon, and yet we see a hard reality near at hand.

The Church recognizes that some marriages do break down and fail. The couple separate, and sometimes they even seek a civil divorce. This is sometimes the only way of ensuring legal rights for one's children or the protection of an inheritance.

The Church continues to love and care for those who divorce. They and their children have suffered one of the most catastrophic experiences imaginable—the breakup of a home and family, the loss of so many hopes and dreams. The Church embraces divorced men and women in this poverty and pain. True, they cannot remarry, because the marriage bond is still there and always will be there. But they are still members of the family. The Church continues to reach out and help all who are separated and divorced, who are struggling to raise their children. They are full members of the family, and the Church wants them to experience the full measure of God's love and mercy. And as long as they do not remarry, they are eligible to receive the Eucharist.

In addition, in some situations, a divorced person can apply for an annulment—which is a legal decision meaning that the marriage never took place because of some deficiency present at the time the marriage was entered into. A parish priest can help guide such people through this process, which many experience as healing.

Our love for those who are suffering should lead us also to do that all we can to prevent such tragedies from happening to others. From the moment a couple take their vows, they should know the support and sincere help of the Church's members. The clergy will do what they can, but this task also falls to the laity—the couple's neighbors, friends, co-workers, and family members. These are usually the "first responders" on the scene when difficulties arise. Priests and deacons are often the last to know.

Young spouses, for their part, should cultivate the habit of seeking advice from experienced and spiritually mature Catholic couples. There is such a wealth of wisdom available in the pews and the vestibules of ordinary Catholic churches. It helps, too, to be active in the parish so that questions come up in the context of ordinary friendship and shared lives.

❖ ❖ ❖ ❖ ❖

Once I asked a long-married couple to tell me the secret of their happiness. The husband jokingly replied, "Oh, I've learned that she's always right." And his wife added, "Yes, and don't you forget it!"

We all laughed together. But then came the touching part. That old gentleman took his wife's hand and said to me, "You know, Bishop, I love her more now than I did the day we were married."

It was enough to bring tears to my eyes. There before me was a beautiful sign of committed love, a public witness for all of us to see. It was a testimony not only of their love but of God's, and in that moment they were ministering to their bishop.

We live in a world where commitment is valued less and less. Employers often feel little obligation to their employees. Civic involvement is in decline, as are voluntary associations.

And many choose to live together so that they do not have to make the commitment to marriage.

We live in a world where love is talked about endlessly, but where endless love is seldom achieved.

But I sense in the younger generation (and by that I mean everyone younger than I am!) a rebellion against the conditions left to them by my generation. In those that come to a church to be married, I sense a sincere search for values, meaning, love, and commitment. Even couples who barely know their faith are hoping for a marriage that lasts, that fulfills them, and that ensures they will be loved to the end of their days.

Those long-married couples testify, by their very lives, that love can indeed bear all things, believe all things, hope all things, endure all things (see 1 Corinthians 13:7).

That's what the Church celebrates in a wedding. That's what the Church celebrates in a marriage. That's the marriage God wants for you.

Bonds of Love

I'd always thought that my wife and I had a good marriage. Both of us came from similar backgrounds, we thought the same way about things that mattered, we had a similar sense of humor, and we enjoyed each other's company. Whenever arguments arose, we made up quickly and got on with life. We had two sons who grew up to be men whom we could be proud of.

Early on, we decided together that I would be the bread-winner of the family. My wife gave up her full-time job as a schoolteacher in order to care for our children. Although we were never going to be rich, we managed to struggle by on one salary. Obstacles there were, but we stuck together and faced them squarely, supporting one another through the bad times.

Then in 2003, after enduring several years of demanding and difficult jobs, I was diagnosed with a complex form of clinical depression. I immediately had to give up my job and essentially could do no work for several years. This seemed to be our biggest trial, yet it was also the event that showed us the true riches of the Sacrament of Marriage. While I sank, irretrievably it seemed, into the pit of despair and spent most days struggling to merely stay alive, my wife never hesitated for an instant. She went back to work, steadfastly trying to pick up her where she had left off in her career as a schoolteacher. It was not easy. We were both in our forties, and work was difficult to come by when there were plenty of younger teachers just coming out of college with all the latest educational theories at their fingertips.

Our marriage vows speak of being faithful to each other in sickness and in health. I have to say that I was astonished and grateful that my wife cheerfully shouldered the burden of the whole family, not only in bringing income into the home, but in sacrificing her free time to look after an inert and largely unresponsive husband who was trapped in his own world of misery. The Sacrament of Marriage, we discovered, really did have power to buoy us up through the difficult and sometimes almost insurmountable struggles of life. It provided the grace we needed to keep loving, not just when things were going well, but through the most harrowing season of our life.

❖   ❖   ❖   ❖   ❖

I am in a difficult marriage. Even though my husband and I have been married for more than twenty years, I know that prayer and the sacraments have given us the grace to stay married.

My husband and I are both broken people. We were raised in divorced and abusive homes, have wrestled with addictions like smoking and drinking, and have mental health issues (I take medication for OCD, and he does for anxiety and depression). My husband has an issue with anger, and when he explodes, my tendency is to show contempt and give him the silent treatment.

I got pregnant while my husband and I were dating; we decided to do the "right" thing and get married. At that time, neither of us was practicing our faith, but we still got married in the Catholic Church. About five years into our marriage, someone gave me a gift subscription to a daily devotional, and I started to have a short prayer time each day. Our family gradually started attending Mass, and I made my first Confession. It didn't go the way I wanted. The priest was very harsh and made me cry. And yet there was a supernatural grace that I received from that Confession, like I was being pieced back together.

Later, I took a chance on a second priest, and he took his time with me and gave me wonderful counsel. I couldn't believe some of the things I was confessing about my negative feelings towards my spouse, and yet the priest just listened. I kept waiting for his condemnation, an accusing sigh, or for his eyes to bug out, but that never happened. Now, Confession is my "go-to" for healing in all my difficult relationships but especially in my marriage.

I believe with all my heart that the Sacrament of Marriage has pulled us along in its loving arms, giving us wings to continually fly back to each other. As my husband and I have been faithful to attending Mass, praying each day, and going to Confession, we have found that God gives us his grace to stay committed to each other and truly love one another! My marriage is still difficult for a variety of reasons, but I have great faith in prayer and the sacraments to lift me up, heal my awful feelings, and recommit me to being a loving spouse.

❖ ❖ ❖ ❖ ❖

Many couples enter marriage expecting their soul mate to fulfill their every need. But no human being can ever completely fulfill another's needs—only God truly completes us. And presuming that my husband will fulfill all of my emotional, spiritual, and social needs is unrealistic at best. It places entirely too much pressure on our marriage relationship and is doomed to failure. I know—I've tried it, and it doesn't work! It also cheats us of the rich wisdom and loving support of our brothers and sisters in Christ.

I now know that there are many things that only other Christian men can give to my husband. I don't have the first idea about how to be a man of God. Similarly, there is insight that I can't get from my husband—I need to get it from other women of God.

My husband and I each have trusted Christian friends with whom we share our lives. I meet every other week with a group of women, and he meets on alternate weeks with a group of men. We don't share details about the other spouse's struggles or divulge information that would make our spouse uncomfortable. But we do share our own real-life joys, sorrows, and questions.

My sisters in this group—and others—have prayed with me for the grace to be the wife and mother God wants me to be. They have listened to me, shared their own journeys, and showed me that I am not alone. They have encouraged me to pray, to go to Confession, and to get reconciled with my husband at times when I was unwilling and unable to listen to him.

There is no such thing as a perfect marriage or a perfect family. Behind closed doors, we all have challenges and need wisdom. God offers us the treasure of brotherhood and sisterhood to give us joy in good times and to sustain us and keep us close to him in bad times. It's true that no man is an island; it's also true that no marriage is an island. We were meant to walk this Christian journey together, with our brothers and sisters. I am so grateful for the body of Christ.

CHAPTER 4

SAINTS IN THE MAKING

Some people have the mistaken impression that "vocation" is a privilege reserved for an elite group of men and women. Some people think that the only Catholics who have vocations are those called to the priesthood or consecrated life.

But that's not true. The truth is that God calls everyone. He calls each and every human person to be a saint. In the Church this is known as "the universal call to holiness." The popes have consistently identified this call as the major theme of the Church's last council, Vatican II (1962–1965)[3]—and thus it is arguably the Church's great message for our time.

We are all called to be saints. Jesus himself issued the call in his Sermon on the Mount. He was addressing the crowd when he said, "So be perfect, just as your heavenly Father is perfect" (Matthew 5:48). He was not laying a burden of perfectionism on the crowd but, rather, he was calling them to share God's life, which is purity, holiness, and love.

Jesus' words were an echo of God's great calling to Israel, given through Moses, to "Be holy, because I am holy" (Leviticus 11:44, 45). The difference is that now, through his saving work, Jesus has given his disciples the power to become God's children (John 1:12), to share in the divine nature (2 Peter

1:4). Human beings cannot be holy on their own, but with God's help they can, because God is holy by nature.

St. Paul said to the Church in Thessalonica, "This is the will of God, your holiness" (1 Thessalonians 4:3). And most of the adults in the congregation he addressed were married men and women.

There is the universal call, and there is a particular call. God calls all men and women to holiness. Some—a small percentage—he calls to be saints through a life of celibacy. But throughout most of history, he has called most Christians to holiness by way of marriage and family life. That is their particular call.

The vocation to marriage has tremendous dignity. Marriage is a sacrament. The family is the primary school of faith. The home is a domestic church, and it is the fundamental building block of both secular society and the Catholic Church. The home and the family—and thus society and the Church—arise from the vocation to marriage.

God calls married couples to walk a well-marked path, which he created to be their road to heaven. They don't walk alone, and they don't go forward in the dark. They follow after generations of saints, they struggle in the company of many other couples, and they walk in the light of Sacred Scripture, Christian Tradition, and the Church's teaching authority.

God wants us to be happy, and he calls us to happiness along the way of our particular vocation. He called me to his priesthood. He called you to marriage. If we are faithful to his call, we will know happiness. You could not be satisfied by following my path, nor could I be satisfied by following yours.

What we have in common is that we want to go to heaven, and for that we must become saints, because only saints live in heaven. When we recite the Creed, we profess our belief in the "communion of saints," and this includes all the population of heaven—all the many saints, some known but most unknown, whom we celebrate on All Saints Day every year.

❖ ❖ ❖ ❖ ❖

In our last chapter, we met St. Augustine, the ancient teacher who spoke so perceptively about the vocation to marriage. In one of the homilies he preached as a bishop, he observed that it's our nature to be satisfied only in a lasting, loving gaze— "to look upon one who looks back in love."[4]

That is the very definition of heaven: to look upon One— almighty God—who looks back in love. And it is the very definition of marriage: to look upon one—the beloved spouse—who looks back in love. For a Christian, then, marriage is a sign and a foretaste of heaven.

We are created in the image and likeness of God (Genesis 1:26-27). The loving gaze of spouses is a sample of God's life and glory.

Just as the path of marriage was created for the salvation of the couple, so each spouse was created precisely for the benefit of the other. As we saw in the story of the creation of

Adam and Eve, husband and wife were designed for mutual help, for complementarity. "As each one has received a gift, use it to serve one another as good stewards of God's varied grace" (1 Peter 4:10). In marriage, even differences can become something holy—"God's varied grace."

As a path to heaven, marriage is a path to happiness. I don't mean to say that we defer happiness until heaven. Quite the contrary: holiness in one's particular state of life means happiness here on earth. It means a clear conscience. It means a mind that's not preoccupied with oneself but rather with care for others. It means inner peace, even in the midst of personal, professional, or social difficulties.

It's important that we understand this well, since our culture presents many false definitions of happiness, and it's easy for us to buy into them. Many people say that happiness is the same thing as pleasure, and it's not. Look into the lives of wayward celebrities who can afford to indulge every stray desire, and you'll usually see profound unhappiness and loneliness. Visit families in impoverished villages in distant lands, on the other hand, and you'll often meet happy, fulfilled people. They have one another and they have love, and they know that love is from God.

The only truly happy marriage is a holy marriage. Holiness does not mean that the husband and wife will never be disappointed, or never be angry, or never struggle with exhaustion or depression. Saints experience all the normal sorrows of ordinary human life, but they don't let their sorrows defeat them. They unite their hardships with the sufferings of Jesus, and they imitate the way he suffered. Jesus learned through suffering (see Hebrews 5:8). St. Paul tells us all, "Have among yourselves the same attitude that is also yours in Christ Jesus,

> Who, though he was in the form of God,
> did not regard equality with God something to be grasped.
> Rather, he emptied himself,
> taking the form of a slave,
> coming in human likeness; . . .
> he humbled himself,
> becoming obedient to death, even death on a cross.
> Because of this, God greatly exalted him
> and bestowed on him the name
> that is above every name. (Philippians 2:5-9)

That vividly describes the love of the heavenly bridegroom for his bride, the Church. It could also describe the self-denying love of so many happy couples you and I have met. Often the wisest and most admirable people we know are those who have suffered much and, like Christ, have come to know a kind of exaltation even on earth.

The way of the cross is the way of Christ and of all the saints. Suffering is an inevitable part of human life. It will be part of marriage too, but it is bearable when husband and wife are striving to bear one another's burdens—striving to carry one another's crosses.

❖ ❖ ❖ ❖ ❖

Maybe you've heard the old saying "No one goes to heaven alone."

The idea is that we're all supposed to bring others along with us, through our example, our acts of kindness, and our words of encouragement and warning. Married people have an advantage in this. They will inevitably have a profound influence on their spouse and the children they raise. If they apply themselves to their vocation—if they strive daily to love—they will model holiness for others, at very close range. And holiness can be contagious up close.

Pope St. John Paul II spoke often of the universal call to holiness, but he sometimes added an additional phrase. He sometimes spoke of the "universal call to holiness *and apostolate*" (emphasis added).[5] "Apostolate" is a technical theological term that simply means religious witness, the spreading of the gospel.

It's good when this is done in sermons from the pulpit, through electronic media, and in Catholic books and magazines. But the first and most effective apostolate is the witness of one spouse to another—and both parents to their children. No preacher or media personality can aspire to the kind of trust that exists naturally in a family. Grace builds beautifully on that kind of nature.

And the witness of a strong family reaches far beyond the walls of the home. It speaks the gospel, wordlessly, to extended family, to neighbors, to schoolmates, to everyone. In previous chapters, I have already spoken about how ordinary married couples have given me new insights into the theology of their vocation. A husband and a wife have extraordinary opportunities to live out their vocation to apostolate. The witness of their lives can be as effective as any homily at delivering the Christian message.

To be Christian is to be called—to holiness and to apostolate. To be married is a particular calling. The glossary of the Church's *Catechism* defines "vocation" like this:

> The calling or destiny we have *in this life and hereafter.* God has created the human person to love and serve him; the fulfillment of this vocation is eternal happiness. Christ calls the faithful to the perfection of holiness. (emphasis added)

Marriage is, for most Christians, the way of Christian life. It is a way to holiness. It is an endless occasion for witness. It begins here and leads us—with others, we pray—to heaven hereafter. It is a calling and a destiny.

Bonds of Love

At a wedding I attended a few years ago, the priest told the bride and groom that by getting married, their job now was to get their spouse (and, God willing, any prospective children) to heaven. I hadn't thought about marriage like that before, but the priest's point crystallized in my mind on a particularly difficult afternoon at home with my two-year-old daughter and infant son.

"Claire is going to be the death of me!" I texted to my husband in a fit of exasperation. I was somewhat joking, but as soon as I hit the "send" button, I realized the truth of that statement. My husband and children give me innumerable opportunities every day (and sometimes throughout the night) to die to myself and put their needs and wants before my own. This is how God is trying to purify me and root out my pride, my desire for control, my impatience, my anger, my selfishness, my sinful human nature. This is how he is going to get me to heaven. After all, as Jesus tells us, "If anyone wishes to come after me, he must deny himself and take up his cross daily and follow me" (Luke 9:23).

This death to self is easy when I take the time to pray, when I get a decent night's sleep, when I am able to get a little "down" time during the day, and, of course, when my children are their sweet, lovable, cheerful little selves. At those times, it feels like the privilege and joy that it truly is to be a wife and mother, to be able to spend my days at home with them, playing games, reading, cuddling together on the couch, and dancing together in the kitchen.

At other times—on the days when there are endless tantrums and time-outs, when I get woken up three or four times during the night by a fussy baby, when I'm frustrated with the monotony of reading the same story for the tenth time—it does feel more like a "cross." Then it becomes more evident that this is how God is drawing me closer to him, giving me countless opportunities to choose to love and to grow in virtue by serving my husband and our children every day.

❖ ❖ ❖ ❖ ❖

They say you should not go into marriage hoping to change your future spouse. A bad habit, a character quirk, or some other trait is all part of the package. "What you see is what you get!" While this is a good observation, it also belies the fact that our Father wants to make us perfect. Jesus teaches, "Be perfect, just as your heavenly Father is perfect" (Matthew 5:48).

When my fiancée became my wife, she got a few surprises. Although there were many things that she loved about me and wouldn't want to change, there were some other things that surfaced in everyday living that weren't so lovable.

My "well of patience" turned out to be a bit too shallow, and I could be quite difficult when I didn't get my way. Angry outbursts happened more than I would have liked. My overreactions often caused unnecessary conflict and hurt feelings.

As I committed to daily personal prayer, however, I became more and more aware of just how much the Father loves me. I realized that my insecurities and childhood wounds were often the source of my overreactions. But I also realized that I am a beloved son of my Father. Over time his love has healed me and deepened my "well of patience."

My own experience of the powerful flood of God's love has also allowed me to see my wife with his eyes and to feel his love for her. Now my own love for her is coming closer to the love that he has for both of us. I am more patient with her imperfections in the way he is patient with mine!

After three decades, our marriage is good and getting better. As we begin anticipating the "empty nest," it is with eyes of wonder that I look forward to spending this next phase of our marriage together. What is God's will for us now? How will he use us for his glory?

I know that Jesus meant what he said in Matthew 5:48 because the Father is constantly providing my wife and me with the grace to be better people than we ever thought we could be. Not perfect yet, but an example that others notice and tell us about.

❖ ❖ ❖ ❖ ❖

In one of Jesus' resurrection appearances, he tells Peter, "When you were younger, you used to dress yourself and go where you wanted; but when you grow old, you will stretch out your hands, and someone else will . . . lead you where you do not want to go" (John 21:18).

This passage can sound grim, but for my wife and me, it has always had a special resonance.

In fact, it is our own kids who are leading us in paths we didn't expect. I'm sure that many parents share this surprise. None of us really knows what to expect when we hold our firstborn child or how much our lives will change now that we have welcomed a new person into our homes. How much more when you are blessed, as we have been, with six children! And how much, much more when all of your children end up having autism or Asperger syndrome, as ours do!

Yes, our kids have led us in ways we never expected: to the waiting rooms of psychologists, psychiatrists, and other therapists; to school conference rooms as we have advocated for them; and to the rocky paths of sleepless nights, full-scale meltdowns, and hours-long struggles over homework, housework, and relationship issues.

Above all, they have led us to our knees in prayer as we beg God to grant them a future in which their gifts are welcomed and where they can make a difference for other people.

According to St. John, Jesus spoke these words to indicate the kind of death that awaited Peter. We have experienced a few little deaths ourselves: the death of our dream for a "Brady Bunch" kind of life and the death of any rigidity we brought to our ideas of parenting.

Perhaps most important has been the death of an overly romanticized take on the spiritual life. Now we know that there are no simple answers and no guaranteed formulas. There is only Jesus' unshakable promise to be with us always. That's the promise we received as we exchanged our wedding vows, and he has never left our side since.

The marriage vocation is meant to be a path to sanctity. For us, that has meant surrender—not defeat, not resignation, but true acceptance. These children are God's exceedingly generous gifts to us. They have taught us so much about ourselves, about the world, and about the Lord. I don't think I'm deceiving myself when I say that I'm a good deal happier now than before I got married— all because I am letting my children lead me to the Lord!

CHAPTER 5

THE EMBODIMENT OF LOVE

The Church's message about sex is more than counter-cultural today—it's practically revolutionary.

We stand now almost fifty years into a society-wide experiment with sexual liberation. Once considered a private matter, sex is today discussed and dissected in nearly every public space—in the media, in the schoolroom, in the laboratory, and on the Internet. It is studied endlessly, uncovered shamelessly, and released from the customs that had marked out its place for centuries.

What our dominant culture offers is sex without consequences, without responsibility, without commitment—and without the precondition of love. In the end, what it delivers is sex without joy.

We are well into the third generation of the experiment that separated sex from marriage and children. And we now live in a culture where divorce is prevalent, where children are born into families without both parents, where many are addicted to pornography. We live amid epidemic levels of loneliness and sexually transmitted diseases. Does anyone really believe the experiment has been good for us?

In such a culture, it's good to be countercultural. It's good, indeed, to be Catholic. That's because the Catholic Church has always spoken the good news about sexual love between a husband and a wife. For many, sexual union is treated as something trivial. But Catholics believe that it is one of God's most magnificent gifts, one of the greatest examples of divine glory in all of creation. For a Catholic, sex is holy, a sign of God's life in all its ecstasy and fruitfulness.

Consider what St. John Chrysostom wrote in the fourth century. First he asked of the husband and wife, "How do they become one flesh?" And then he answered his rhetorical question: "As if she were gold receiving purest gold, the woman receives the man's seed with rich pleasure, and within her it is nourished, cherished, and refined. It is mingled with her own substance and she then returns it as a child!" As a result, he said, marriage becomes a sign of the Trinity: "The child is a bridge connecting mother to father, so the three become one flesh. . . . And here the bridge is formed from the substance of each!"[6]

In modern times, we have come to call such reflection the "theology of the body." But it is really as old as the gospel. As Catholics, we believe that the sexual union of spouses, when it is lived with integrity, speaks a profound truth about God.

❖ ❖ ❖ ❖ ❖

This saving truth is so important that it is preserved in the very first pages of the Scriptures honored by all Jews and Christians. In the opening chapters of the Book of Genesis, we learn that God created the human race in two complementary sexes.

Men and women were made for one another, and they were made in the divine image (see Genesis 1:26-28 and 2:21-25).

What does that mean? It means that like God, human beings have the capacity to love, to enter into relationship with one another. This is something distinctively human. Animals *mate*, according to their instinct, but they do not *love* because it is not in their nature. Unlike us, they lack the spiritual capacity to know another and love another.

We are human because we can love, and we can love because we are created to be like God in precisely that way.

Our love, of course, is much more limited than God's. God is eternal love, perfect love, infinite love. Within the Trinity, the Father loves the Son completely and gives himself entirely to him. The Son returns that love in equal measure by the gift of himself. The Holy Spirit is the love shared by both the Father and the Son. Their eternal communion is infinite love, and all creation is an expression of its abundance and overflow.

We are made from such lavish love, and we are made to share that love forever in heaven. Even now, however, even as we live on earth, we reflect God's love in our entire being.

God made each human person a unity of body and soul—a material body and a spiritual soul. Our interior spiritual realities reflect the God who made us, the God who is pure spirit. But our bodies also express our spiritual identity, and thus the human body is a physical image of God in the world.

This fact has profound consequences for everyday life. It is especially relevant to any consideration of the physical union of marriage.

It means that the body is made for faithfulness, as God is faithful. It means that the body is made for constancy in marriage, as God has remained constant with his Church. It means that the body is made for loving one spouse—and only one's spouse—as Christ loves the Church, and the Church loves Christ alone. It means also that the body is made for fruitfulness, as God is lavish in his gifts to us, both in the natural and supernatural orders.

The sacred author tells us that in the beginning, "the man and his wife were both naked, yet they felt no shame" (Genesis 2:25). That is how God intends sexual union, in all its integrity, to be. An inseparable part of this creation, however, is God's command to the first couple: "Be fertile and multiply; fill the earth and subdue it" (Genesis 1:28). The couple's sexual relationship, and each sexual act, are to be open to life—open to God's creative act.

With the creation of Adam and Eve, God established the norm and pattern of human marriage. So important is that passage in Genesis that it is cited repeatedly and in significant ways by Jesus and, later, by St. Paul (see Mark 10:8; 1 Corinthians 6:16; and Ephesians 5:31).

❖ ❖ ❖ ❖ ❖

God made Adam, the first man, and declared his creation to be "very good." Yet it was still lacking something. Even though it was "very good," it was not good enough. We know this because Adam still longed for completion. God declared, then, that it was not good for the man to be alone, and so he created a helpmate, an equal, a partner for Adam, someone who would be his constant companion.

Adam's longing is universal. It is natural to desire a loving, lasting relationship with another person. We are social beings, and we are created for relationship.

The suitability of men for women, and women for men, is evident in the design of the human body. Male and female were created with bodily differences that are complementary.

In fulfilling Adam's longing, Eve completes her husband, just as Adam completes Eve. That is a pattern followed in every sacramental marriage. And it is, as the Creator declared, *very good* (Genesis 1:31). Faithfulness, fruitfulness, and openness to the amazing adventure of God's will: these qualities make for a rich life, no matter the material circumstances.

Yet that is only the beginning. All of those good things are a sign of a far greater reality. They represent our relationship with God and God's desire to complete whatever is lacking in us.

The Catholic vision of love—a vision that has been proven successful over thousands of years—is radically different from that of our culture. Unfortunately, the vision of love prevalent in our culture today not only changes from year to year, but has wreaked havoc on family life and society.

No matter what the sitcoms and advice columns tell us, sex is not made to be a mild form of recreation. It is not a drug to be indulged in and then put aside. It is a mighty force of nature—like the tides and shifts of the earth's tectonic plates—and it should be respected as such. It is a sign more powerful than all the miracles of Jesus' earthly ministry. It calls for a measure of trust in God. It calls for a measure of gratitude. It calls for complete integrity.

It is unbroken Christian tradition, the clear teaching of the Catholic Church, that every sexual act should belong within marriage, and that every sexual act should be loving, fully consensual, and open to life.

Jesus holds up for us the original plan for human sexuality. He restores the dignity of the couple and restores them to a condition of true love, that they may be "naked and without shame"(see Genesis 2:25).

This is the true revolution. For those who choose it and live it faithfully, it promises glorious consequences, not only for today, but for their old age as well as for generations in the future. With faithfulness come responsibility, commitment, security, love—and God's grace and a peaceful conscience.

Nothing less is worthy of the marriage that God wants for you.

Bonds of Love

Our oldest child was just finishing up eighth grade when I found myself expecting again. What a shock! I was forty years old and we already had five children. I couldn't believe that my oldest and youngest would be fourteen years apart!

I remember feeling self-conscious being the only mother waddling through my daughter's freshman orientation for high school in the fall. I thought, "All these parents are near the end of their parenting, and I am starting over again!"

As with most hard things in my life, I turned to the Lord. I've learned the hard way that worry and panic don't solve anything. What does help is having a regular prayer time. By grounding myself in God's love for me and his word, I get so much encouragement. I personally need a lot of encouragement because I am an only child from a divorced family, and I often wonder if I am doing things "right."

I go to Confession regularly because I know God makes all things new. I needed this during my last pregnancy more than ever. I would often tell the Lord, "I'm not so new anymore, and what am I doing going through this again?"

Some close sisters in Christ helped me get my house ready for baby number six. Although I thought that my church community would not support our family with meals for yet *another* baby, we received twenty-two meals from family and friends, which only confirmed for me that God will provide with every child.

This fortieth-birthday "surprise" is now six years old, and I am so glad he is here! He has brought much joy to our family and keeps my husband and me feeling young. We're the oldest parents in his kindergarten class, and we love it. We don't have to worry about things that concern the other parents because we have been through this five times before.

My husband and I are so grateful that we've been open to new life throughout our twenty-year marriage. We tend to be opposites in many ways, but in this area we have always been in agreement. God has blessed us through each pregnancy and birth and has carried us through every difficulty. May God be praised! We thank him for his wisdom, his guidance, and his gift of life.

❖ ❖ ❖ ❖ ❖

When Liz and I were first married, we had our dreams, as most newly wedded couples do. I was older, so we thought that three children would be the right-sized family for us. We also knew that we wanted to stay faithful to the Church's teaching on artificial contraception. We had read *Humanae Vitae* together and were moved by the beautiful portrait of married life that Blessed Paul VI had painted. We wanted to express our love for each other in the pure, chaste way described in this encyclical, challenging though it might be at times.

Little did we know that surrendering ourselves to the Lord in this way would be so demanding! I'm not talking about the periods of abstinence that are crucial to Natural Family Planning. Liz and I are pretty disciplined people, and we looked at these times as opportunities to love each other in different, more creative ways. No, the challenge for us was the three "surprise" pregnancies. In nine years, we were blessed with six children! Clearly, NFP wasn't working for us, no matter how diligent we were. But looking back, I can see God's hand at work.

With each surprise pregnancy, Liz and I knew we had a choice. We could get angry at God for not "playing by the rules," or we could embrace his plan for us with trusting and generous hearts. We also had the choice to disregard the Church's clear teaching on the regulation of birth, or we could continue to trust that the Lord was speaking through his Church. It wasn't always easy, and there were times when we were sorely tempted to choose a different path—especially when the bills came due and when one or the other of us began to feel overwhelmed by the demands of a large family.

But each time we faced these temptations, the Lord helped us through them—mainly through our children. "Look at him," Liz would say to me, pointing to one of our little "surprises." "Could you imagine him not being a part of us?" No, we couldn't imagine it. Each child is God's special gift to us.

Medical complications after our sixth child was born ended our fertility. But I know we have exactly the number of children God wanted to give us. Liz and I had planned on giving each other three children, but, as in so many other areas of lives, our God is far more generous than we could ever be.

CHAPTER 6

More Than a Feeling

Marriages are more likely to thrive when both spouses keep mindful of certain paradoxes. A paradox is a statement that seems to contradict itself but is nonetheless true. Consider these two:

(1) It should not be surprising that every marriage comes with surprises.
(2) One thing that doesn't change is the fact that people change.

Change is inevitable. It marks the milestones along our way to growth and maturity. And it rarely takes place exactly as we had planned or expected. Blessed John Henry Newman said, "To live is to change, and to be perfect is to have changed often."[7]

In marriages, spouses make a commitment to stay with one another through all the changes, all the ups and downs, and all the changes in weather, fortune, and feelings.

Life's changes often present the greatest challenges to happiness in a relationship. Events change us. When spouses have children, it's a great joy, but it also changes who they are. They become something different—they become parents. Suddenly there is another personal presence constantly in their thoughts, affecting their sleep and influencing their choices from moment to moment.

The birth of a child leads to dramatic changes, but they are hardly the only ones. We all experience sorrows as we grow older. We lose loved ones—grandparents, parents, and friends—and we grieve for the loss. Their absence can change a person just as much as the presence of a newborn child.

We are affected as well by changes in circumstance: promotions or demotions at work, for example, or the relocation from one place to another. These can shake us up in profound and unexpected ways, introducing new stresses, new demands on our time, and new energy or drains on our energy.

Our bodies change too over time, and this will affect the way we look and the way we eat and sleep. Bodily changes can also affect the way we experience our emotions and passions.

The truth is that relationships also change. This is demonstrably true of our friendships and relationships with co-workers, but it's true also of our close family relationships. We relate to our parents in different ways at different stages. When we were toddlers, we related one way; when we were teenagers, our interactions became very different. As we grew into adulthood, they became something else entirely. Constant through it all was a bond of love that was impervious to these changes. Our parents cannot cease to be our parents, and we do not cease to be their children.

The marriage bond is even stronger than that, and it remains constant through the many changes in feelings, circumstances, and emotions. The bond itself is not a feeling, and it is not dependent on any feeling. Feelings come and go; they come back, and they go again. But the marital bond remains for the duration of life. It is a still point in a changing world.

❖   ❖   ❖   ❖   ❖

Passions, of course, often play a decisive role in the relationship between a man and a woman. The passions can be fueled by physical attraction and the newness of an emerging friendship. So many factors play into the drama of romantic love. There is, at first, an elemental curiosity about someone who is deeply different from oneself—different in life experiences, different in interests, different in body and mind. These are the details that find their way into love letters, love songs, romantic poems, and Valentine's Day cards.

We associate passion with love, especially at the beginning of a relationship. But we should be careful not to *equate* passion with love, because they're very different things.

As human beings, we experience many passions, and each of them has a purpose. God gave us our passions to move us toward good things. Anger is a passion, for example. Its purpose is to drive us to seek justice and right wrongs. Anger often provides the first impulse, the first movement toward great social change. Yet we know that anger can be overvalued, overindulged in, or abused. It must be restrained and disciplined if it is to be truly effective for good.

Romantic feelings, too, are a passion. Their purpose is to draw two people together to form a family. Romance has also inspired some of the greatest works of literature, art, and music. In forming families, it cannot help but build up a noble culture as well.

Romantic passion serves great purposes. Yet like any other passion, it can be overvalued and misdirected. It is a stage in the way of love. It is not the entirety of the way.

Passions serve their purpose. Feelings rise and fall. But married love remains constant. It is something objectively real and lasting. When we can't see a particular mountain or ocean because of fog or nightfall, we know it is still there. Well, marriage has the same kind of permanence.

People sometimes speak of "falling in love"—and the phrase has poetic power. When a man and a woman are caught by the passion of romance and attraction, they sometimes feel helpless. The force seems as strong as gravity or the tides. The effect seems as unpreventable and unstoppable as a sudden fall.

We should take exception, however, when anyone speaks of a married couple as "falling out of love." As we have already said, married love is a vocation from God. It arrives with grace and power from God. Therefore, it is not fleeting. People cannot "fall" out of it. There is no power in the natural world that can make someone fall out of love. Married love is created by God to endure all things and never fail or end (see 1 Corinthians 13:7-8).

When spouses fear that they are falling out of love, they should take care to distinguish their feelings and passions from their commitment. When they pray, they should call upon the grace of the sacrament, and God will surely respond because "love is of God" (1 John 4:7). Listen to Pope Francis:

> The love of Christ, which has blessed and sanctified the union of husband and wife, is able to sustain their love and to renew it when, humanly speaking, it becomes lost, wounded, or worn out. The love of Christ can restore to spouses the joy of journeying together.[8]

And it's true. The Lord said to St. Paul what he will say to anyone who struggles with vocational commitment: "My grace is sufficient for you, for power is made perfect in weakness" (2 Corinthians 12:9).

God will give the grace needed for love to endure, even as feelings change. This grace may lead a couple to seek counsel from clergy or other professionals. I strongly urge anyone who seeks such help to insist upon professionals who understand and uphold the Catholic view of marriage.

Married love is a grace, a gift from God. A man and a woman may feel they're falling into it. But staying in it requires a decision. God wants us to correspond freely to every grace given to us. So love is a decision that must be made repeatedly.

The failure to love is also a decision. It usually begins with a decision *not* to pray, *not* to forgive, *not* to apologize, or *not* to put the other's wishes before one's own. Such a failure is more truly a fall, and it can leave a spouse—or both spouses—feeling weak and more helpless as time passes.

In those moments, God is especially present, especially near, awaiting repentance and always ready to grant the graces needed for healing.

Repentance—with the acceptance of grace—is an important part of love, and it is a decision that must be made again and again. So too is it important that husbands and wives continually seek the forgiveness of one another. Only through mutual forgiveness will a marriage thrive and last.

❖   ❖   ❖   ❖   ❖

It's not something we like to think about—it's not something anyone can really plan for—but every marriage faces sorrows, challenges, trials, and suffering. Even these, however, need not defeat a loving husband and wife. They are, in fact, essential to all the great love stories in history.

Alice Middleton married one of the most prominent lawyers in England. Thomas More was a member of parliament and undersheriff of the city of London, and his star was still rising. He was a virtuous man, charitable and just, and widely admired. There seemed no possible obstacle to his future glory. People expected him to go far, and he did not disappoint them. He rose, eventually, to become Lord Chancellor of England, in power and influence second only to the king.

Alice could not have foreseen the strange turn of events in her husband's future. King Henry VIII sought to annul his marriage to the queen, Catherine of Aragon, and marry another woman, Anne Boleyn. When the pope did not grant an annulment, Henry declared himself to be the supreme head of the Church in England.

Thomas More, alone among his colleagues in government, found he could not support the king's actions, and so he quietly withdrew from public life—a move that plunged his family into poverty and effectively ended Thomas's career. Eventually, the king came to demand Thomas's public support; Thomas refused and was imprisoned.

Alice suffered greatly from Thomas's decisions. She admitted to her husband that she did not understand the legal, philosophical, or moral issues he faced. But she respected him, trusted him, and stood by him in his difficulties.

Eventually, Thomas was executed for treason for his refusal to recognize the king's marriage and his claim to be supreme head over the Church. Thomas died, in fact, a martyr for the honor of marriage.

And Alice, in her way, gave testimony for the same cause. Her loyalty and love were exemplary. Her marriage to Thomas remained strong and happy, even through those final years of difficulty and separation.

King Henry, on the other hand, went from bad to worse. He executed Anne Boleyn just one year after the beheading of Thomas More. Henry would go on to "marry" four more women in quick succession before dying in misery.

Thomas More, on the other hand, was cheerful as he went to his death. In time he was canonized a saint by the Church.

He and his wife have left us, moreover, a love story for the ages, because they were true to God and true to one another, in spite of the sorrows that took them by surprise.

❖   ❖   ❖   ❖   ❖

Staying true in the midst of surprising sorrows: that is the story of couples in strong, loving marriages. It is probably the story of the long-married couples you most admire.

They're not "perfect" couples, you can be sure, because there's no such thing. Thomas and Alice, who loved one another till death, were not a perfect couple. But successful husbands and wives are those who learn to live with one another's imperfections. Each learns to be a source of strength for the other, making up for the other's particular weaknesses, while knowing that the other is doing the same.

The love that every bride and groom longs for is much more than a feeling, much more than a passion. What, then, is it? Pope Francis asks the same question, and then he answers it for us in a memorable way.

But what do we mean by "love"? Is it only a feeling, a psycho-physical state? Certainly, if that is it, then we cannot build on anything solid. But if, instead, love is a relationship, then it is a reality that grows, and we can also say by way of example that it is built up like a home. And a home is built together, not alone! To build something here means to foster and aid growth.

Dear engaged couples, you are preparing to grow together, to build this home, to live together forever. You do not want to found it on the sand of sentiments, which come and go, but on the rock of true love, the love that comes from God. The family is born from this plan of love; it wants to grow just as a home is built, as a place of affection, of help, of hope, of support. As the love of God is stable and forever, should we want the love on which a family is based to be stable and forever.[9]

Bonds of Love

I can still recall quite vividly how I felt walking into the retreat house the weekend of our Engaged Encounter. My husband and I have reflected on it many times throughout our marriage, and it always brings us back to that "warm and fuzzy" feeling that seemed to surround us in those days! We could never have imagined then how our lives would change, mostly for the better, but not without some major struggles and sorrows along the way. And it was during those difficult times when that one piece of advice, summed up in a single sentence, became most valuable: love is a decision.

Those four words carried us through the lean years as we worked hard to climb out of debt. They sustained us during the numbing sorrow of multiple miscarriages and the aftermath of grief that had the potential to render us as strangers living side by side. It brought us through too many angry outbursts and too few signs of affection, as well as the day-to-day stresses that can culminate in superficial conversation and unspoken tension.

And this has brought about something extraordinary: a love with roots deeper than feelings and with wings that carry us higher than our present circumstances. It has blessed us with a love that blossoms in spite of bad weather or "desert conditions." My husband and I now share a love that speaks even in the silence and shines even in the dark. It is a love sustained by grace and the choice, freely made and given one day at a time, for twenty-five years and counting!

❖   ❖   ❖   ❖   ❖

During our engagement, I expressed to my husband-to-be my desire to pray together regularly. He took that request to heart, and we began praying together every day, even if only by telephone. We carried that practice into our marriage. We began praying together when we went to bed, offering an Our Father and our petitions for our family and friends.

But praying at night, after a full day of work and then evening activities, was not the best time for us. Sometimes we even fell asleep in the middle of our prayers! Several months ago, we were led to deepen our prayer together. Inspired by a seminar we had attended that encouraged daily Scripture reading and reflection as a couple, we began rising a half hour earlier each day to pray together.

So now our prayer as a couple usually centers on the daily Mass readings, followed by our reading of a meditation from a daily devotional or listening to a short podcast. Then we share our own thoughts about the Scripture readings. Sometimes our prayer time is an occasion for asking and receiving forgiveness from one another. We still pray for our own needs and those of others and conclude with the Lord's Prayer.

God has blessed our resolution to offer him the first-fruits of our day. We have developed a habit, and now we look forward to starting each day this way. It helps us maintain a loving attitude toward each other because it is hard to pray with someone you are at odds with! We even prayed together each morning during a recent vacation with extended family. In the past, praying while traveling with others has been a challenge. This time we found that making it a priority gave us a much more restful vacation.

I thank God that my request for daily prayer with my husband has been answered in such a tangible way.

CHAPTER 7

UNITY: A TOUCH OF THE TRINITY

Jesus' most extended teaching on the Holy Eucharist—indeed, one of his most extensive teachings on any subject—is his Bread of Life discourse found in chapter 6 of St. John's Gospel. He uses graphic language as he explains the sacrament. He wants the people to know that he is not simply waxing poetic or using metaphors. There's a vivid realism in the terms he chooses, and his language gets stronger the more his listeners challenge him.

They say, "What sign can you do, that we may see and believe in you?" (John 6:30). They want him to feed their bellies with bread. Jesus, however, wants to give them something far better. He replies, "I am the bread of life" (6:35).

His listeners murmur and grumble because Jesus is not offering them what they want. He is offering them something infinitely better, but they do not understand.

Still, Jesus presses on, speaking with greater clarity, even though his language frightens the crowd: "I am the living bread that came down from heaven; whoever eats this bread will live forever; and the bread that I will give is my flesh for the life of the world" (John 6:51).

He will not back down from the truth, even though it seems too difficult—and even too good—to be true. They call it a "hard saying" (cf. John 6:50). St. John tells us that "many of his disciples" left him that day. They "returned to their former way of life and no longer accompanied him" (6:66).

This is how it goes when Jesus talks about the sacraments. Some people choose to listen, and they draw abundant life from his doctrine. Others walk away. Sadly, "many" walk away and "no longer accompany him."

It is no less true of Jesus' doctrine of the Sacrament of Matrimony. In fact, at the end of his most extensive teaching on the subject, his disciples respond in exactly the same way as they had responded to his discourse on the Bread of Life! "If that is the case," they say, "it is better not to marry" (Matthew 19:10).

Sacraments are shocking. They promise us heaven. They signify heaven. They deliver heaven. But they also make demands on us. They do things that literary symbols can never do.

Marriage, like the Eucharist, is not a mere symbol or metaphor. It is a sign woven by the Creator into the very fabric of creation. God makes his "metaphors" not just with words, but with the things of the world. You and I may invoke the stars or the moon as figures of speech, but God created the stars and the moon to stand forever as signs of his power.

Marriage, because it is a sacrament, is a sign far more powerful than the sun or the moon or the stars. It is not some kind of quaint custom or social convention. It is a unique and irreplaceable revelation of God's inner life.

It is a mystery that should shake us and strike awe in our hearts. The ex-disciples who rejected Jesus understood that much, at least. They understood it perhaps better than people today, who hear about the Church's teaching on marriage and then smirk or shrug. Those long-ago listeners knew that Jesus' words, if true, implied life-changing consequences.

If marriage were to reveal divine life to the world—and bring divine life to the world—then the lives of those who are married would need to change. Indeed, marriage itself would need to change them in a radical way.

❖ ❖ ❖ ❖ ❖

How on earth can marriage reveal God? How, in heaven's name, can marriage manifest and mediate the Trinity? The task seems too great to be borne—like asking bread and wine to become God's Body and Blood.

Yet so it is. We have learned the terms of the sacraments from God in the flesh, Jesus Christ.

The saints are those who receive Jesus' words with joy. In previous chapters, we have seen how saints, from John Chrysostom to John Paul II, have understood the "sign" of marriage. The ancient faith has not been diminished over time. Pope Francis has echoed our forebears in terms as strong as Jesus' own. In marriage, he says, the two achieve a real and profound unity.

When a man and woman celebrate the Sacrament of Matrimony, God as it were "is mirrored" in them; he impresses in them his own features and the indelible character of his love. Marriage is the icon of God's love for us. Indeed, God is communion too: the three Persons of the Father, the Son, and the Holy Spirit live eternally in perfect unity. And this is precisely the mystery of matrimony: God makes of the two spouses one single life. The Bible uses a powerful expression and says "one flesh," so intimate is the union between man and woman in marriage. And this is precisely the mystery of marriage: the love of God which is reflected in the couple that decides to live together. Therefore a man leaves his home, the home of his parents, and goes to live with his wife and unites himself so strongly to her that the two become—the Bible says—one flesh.[10]

This is how God most effectively reveals his eternal unity to the world. Not through volumes of theology and not through long sermons, but rather through the sign of marriage—through the public witness of the life of a loving couple.

A married couple's God-like unity is a grace of the sacrament. The Trinity bestows unity upon those whom God touches sacramentally. We see this effect in Baptism, which unites believers in faith (see Ephesians 4:5). We see it in the Eucharist, which makes the Church "one bread, one body" (see 1 Corinthians 10:17). We see it in Confirmation, where the Spirit makes us to share "one Spirit" with Christ (see 1 Corinthians 6:17).

The unity of a married couple gives testimony to the grace they have received. Such couples have come to share the life of God—and it is our privilege to *see* what they have been given. They have been given the very life of God.

As St. Augustine said many centuries ago, "If you see love, you see the Trinity."[11]

The saints are those who are willing to accept the sacraments on Jesus' terms. We recognize the Lord's doctrine in the preaching of St. John Chrysostom and Pope St. John Paul. But I'm not speaking only of the canonized saints.

I am speaking also of those many couples you and I encounter as we go about our lives. I am speaking about those many couples who come to the Church to celebrate their milestone anniversaries with me. It is no accident that in recent years, I have celebrated their Mass on the Solemnity of the Most Blessed Trinity—"Trinity Sunday." The couples themselves become a most eloquent homily for the feast day.

Their lives are beautiful, but they have not been easy. Some have had to struggle together to overcome addictions. Some have endured long separations from one another. Some have suffered the loss of a child. Some have passed through devastating illnesses. And yet they have arrived, united, to mark that special day—and they are committed to marking as many more as God will grant.

This is what the Trinity accomplishes in the Church, through the Spirit, by means of the sacrament.

❖　❖　❖　❖　❖

As in the Church, so in the family children are born, and the family is united around a table. Birth brings life in a family, and natural nourishment fosters family communion.

And just as in the Church, so in the family unity does not mean uniformity. Husband and wife bring different gifts and different perspectives to their shared life. They should recognize their differences, respect them, and even celebrate them. Spouses should strive to live in a way that's not oppositional but rather complementary. I have known loving couples who differ passionately about politics, food preferences, sports teams, and many other things. It does not diminish their love but rather enhances it.

I recall, many years ago, reading about a famous French Catholic couple, Jacques and Raissa Maritain. They were both philosophers, and they loved one another deeply. Once when they were very young, they had a disagreement, and they couldn't bear the pain of it. They vowed that they would always, from that moment on, find a way to mutual agreement in everything. While their love is admirable, I'd say it is also exceptional. Most couples live peaceably with many differences. Many come to realize, gradually over time, that they have come to love one another's differences.

There are differences that matter and differences that don't. It is, of course, important to make that distinction. We do not want to encourage a predilection for sin or vice, for example, in the people we love. Those we should overcome by prayer and kindness.

Consider the life of Élisabeth Arrighi. She married a man, Felix Leseur, who was a committed atheist and quite hostile to the Catholic faith. The difference didn't seem important to her when she was young because her own faith was not very strong. But his anti-Catholic arguments actually drove her to learn the faith, and when she learned it, she came to love it. As she loved the faith, she became a better person. She loved Felix all the more and all the better.

While still relatively young, Élisabeth became ill with cancer. Felix saw his beloved wife face death with great serenity.

When she died, he learned from her journals that she had been praying for him for many years. Her prayers worked; her love changed him. Not only did Felix become a practicing Catholic; he entered the Dominican order and eventually became a priest. The Church is today considering Élisabeth Leseur's cause for sainthood.

So, yes, some differences matter; but even those differences can be overcome with love that is touched by the Trinity in the Sacrament of Matrimony. Because, as St. Paul noted, "Love is patient, love is kind" (1 Corinthians 13:4).

❖   ❖   ❖   ❖   ❖

"We worship one God in Trinity, and Trinity in Unity, neither confounding the Persons, nor dividing the Essence." So runs one of the Church's ancient creeds. We say that God is three divine Persons, yet those three are somehow one. It seems impossible simply on mathematical terms. How can three be indivisibly one?

And yet that is the faith that many thousands of people came to accept when it was quite illegal to do so. That is the faith that many millions of people have come to profess and proclaim down the centuries.

Many great minds have applied themselves to the explanation and elucidation of the mystery: Augustine, Aquinas, Anselm, and Bonaventure, to name just a few. Theologians continue to apply themselves to the task in our own day.

Yet all their efforts will pale before the witness of a strong marriage, a human plurality in sacramental unity, bound by charity.

Theology bows before the reality of the marriage God wants for you.

Bonds of Love

My husband and I have walked down many dark roads through the years, but we have always managed to find a way to stay on the path hand in hand. This time we were facing a debilitating medical issue with our daughter that left her curled up in bed in pain and unable to walk.

We were weathering the multiple doctor visits, the wheelchair, and the possibility that this might be the "new normal." But the toughest time for us came because of my daughter's needs at night, when I would sleep on a futon next to her bed to calm her anxiety.

That time at her bedside ripped away at the lifeline to our marriage—our only chance for private conversation about medical updates, decision making, and balancing the needs of our other kids. That lack of nightly communication started to starve our marriage of its necessary nutrition.

Although we would do our best to overcome this lack of time for communicating, it was never enough. That's when I noticed that my prayers began to change. I no longer prayed only for the big healing miracle or that my husband would see things "my way." Instead, I found myself praying that whatever the Lord wanted us to do, he would put it in both of our minds very clearly. In effect, I was calling on the grace that flows from the sacrament of our marriage to have the Lord give us a united mind.

And God answered my prayer in an amazing way. When we described to some friends how our daughter was withering away day by day, they recommended that we have a priest come and give her the Sacrament of the Anointing of the Sick. Immediately, my husband and I jumped at the idea and had a priest come to anoint our daughter.

Within the next two weeks, we heard about some medical options that we didn't know existed. We both felt united to try them, despite their large price tag, and the treatments resulted in answers and a full healing of our daughter. Without a united mind and the sacraments, I can't imagine what our life would be like today.

The lesson that we learned left us both with a solemn sense of awe and wonder at God's love for us and our marriage. Now I know that when we face a big decision, we need to let God guide us and wait until we come to a united decision. Even though we don't agree on everything, I can count on the Lord—and the grace of our sacrament—to have the united answer for us when it's the direction that God wants us to take.

❖   ❖   ❖   ❖   ❖

The question often posed to couples—"Do you pray together?"—has many layers of meaning. It can be answered with a simple "Yes. We pray before meals, when we get in the car, when one of our children is in trouble."

But prayer is not just something we do, whether it is a form prayer, a Scripture sharing, or something more spontaneous that goes beyond words. Prayer flows from an intense awareness of our marriage as a spiritual and physical reality that is grounded in the abiding presence of God. So for my husband and me, the answer to that question is "Yes. We often acknowledge Father, Son, and Holy Spirit, the source of our unity and love." Let me share an example.

Our first home was in a small Midwestern town, a great place to raise our growing family. My husband, Ray, had what began as the ideal job in his field. But after a few years, serious administrative issues began to emerge and worsen.

Ray began to talk about a national job search. As we started to pray together, I was adamant about staying put. I did not want to uproot the children and go back to living in rental property in a city. But Ray's work situation was deteriorating, so he asked me to pray about it by myself as well.

So I turned to Jesus often. "Don't you care about what we need, God? Can't Ray just change careers and find something nearby?" Still, at the end of every anxious tirade, I surrendered myself and our family to God. Then one day I remembered another time when Ray had known it was time to leave a job. I had to admit that Ray was right then and was probably right now. So I prayed, "God, I trust Ray. And I trust you to lead me through him. Amen."

Many times since then, I have surrendered my own desires in prayer and laid them alongside what Ray hears in prayer, knowing we can both encounter God's mercy and a new unity. As St. Francis de Sales observed in his *Introduction to the Devout Life*, "If two pieces of wood are carefully glued together, their union will be so close that it is easier to break them in some fresh place than where they were joined; and God so unites man and wife, that it is easier to sever soul and body than the two."

❖ ❖ ❖ ❖ ❖

A few years ago, my wife and I planned a ten-day trip to Rome. This was going to be an amazing trip, away from all of our responsibilities at work, away from kids and everything that involves, and a time of focusing upon our faith and one another.

My wife knows me and I know her, and the gift of a committed marriage is the gift of familiarity. Once we landed, that knowledge brought her to the correct realization that I was not interested in following a map as we walked about Rome; rather, she knew that I would want to wander in and out of shops, being surprised by all of the churches and vendors along the way. But such a free-spirit type of approach to travel drives my wife crazy. She needs a "to do" list in order to feel like she hasn't wasted her day. So what could we do? If we were unwilling to be flexible with one another, our trip could end up with memories of numerous arguments.

We decided that there would be at least two things a day that we set out to accomplish from her list, and for the rest of the time we could meander about here and there. As long as we were heading toward completing one of the tasks on our list, we didn't have to be on a mad dash trying to hit every tourist "must see" throughout the entire day. This decision made for an amazing time in Rome. It helped our time together to be what it was meant to be: renewing, refreshing, and memorable.

We need to be pliable and enjoy the gifts and ways our spouse approaches things, even if they are different from our own. The more we can appreciate what the other enjoys, the greater our possibilities, not only for adventure, but also for avoiding a lot of conflict.

The Church invites us to realize that true grace is present for the couple to grow in sanctity, including the grace to say yes to one another's differences and unique qualities. Marriage is more than just two people coming together because they have an attraction toward one another. It also means laying down our own wants and desires for the sake of the other. And by growing in love in that way, we have the chance to model the love of the Trinity.

CHAPTER 8

TURNING TO THE RITE

The preparations for marriage are usually extensive, and the celebration itself is a moment of great joy, not only for the couple, but also for their families and friends. It should be this way, because a marriage marks the beginning of two lives coming together as a whole new reality—a new family, the shared life of wife and husband.

It has been my privilege to preside at many weddings in my fifty years of priesthood. I have served as a priest and bishop on the two coasts of North America as well as in Europe, so I have seen the rich diversity of customs that Catholics associate with the couple's great day. These traditions vary by region, by ethnicity, and sometimes even by family.

At the heart of the day, however, is the rite we all hold in common. The word "catholic" comes from the Greek word for "universal." We are many, but we are united by a common faith and sacramental life, and this is expressed in our common worship. We refer to the Church's ritual public worship as "liturgy." It's another word we take from the Greek (meaning "public work"), and for many people it is unfamiliar. One of my jobs as a priest, however, is to help the couple—far in advance of their wedding day—become familiar not only with the word but with the rite as well.

A Catholic wedding is a public event. It follows a certain traditional form that is recognized by the Church throughout the entire world. A Catholic wedding is rich in meaning, history, and symbolism. It exercises a power that is both natural and supernatural. It affects—and it evangelizes—not only the couple, but all those who attend the ceremony.

Christians should always strive to worship in a mindful way, and that is especially true at a wedding, when vows are exchanged and informed consent is essential. When I meet with a couple to plan for their wedding, we talk about many things. We discuss their future married life, of course, but we also speak in great detail about their marriage's beginning: their wedding and what it means.

❖   ❖   ❖   ❖   ❖

I sometimes have to begin by explaining—or even defending—the very idea of ritual. Let me take a moment to offer such an explanation here.

In secular culture today, many people question the meaning of marriage, and so they are reluctant to impose any limits on the form of a wedding. In some places, civil authorities will even permit couples to write their own vows, which can be open-ended or loaded down with qualifications to suit the preferences, fears, and eccentricities of each party to the contract.

Catholic liturgy *cannot* proceed that way. The Church—in every place and in every age—professes a common faith, a certain faith, a particular faith, which includes a clear doctrine of marriage. The Church's faith is reflected in all the words, gestures, and symbols of its liturgy. A Catholic wedding is a public event with legal, lifelong, and covenantal effects. So it is important that the couple and their witnesses have an *objective* standard that is universally recognized within the Church, a standard they can use to hold one another accountable. Again, that standard is reflected in the Rite of Marriage and especially in the exchange of vows.

A couple can choose from many options to express what is unique or special about their relationship. They can choose from many Scripture readings. They can select from a vast tradition of hymns and sacred music. They can incorporate particular traditional devotions to Jesus Christ and the Blessed Virgin Mary. But it is important that their vows be those that are recognized by the Catholic Church, reflecting what the Catholic Church believes and professes regarding marriage. If the vows take place within the context of a nuptial Mass, then the Mass also must follow the ritual form prescribed by the Church.

Some people today look down upon ritual. They speak as if it is a synonym for *mechanical*, *rote*, or even *mindless*. But that's a false notion. The truth is that we observe rituals for many of the important things in life. Every day we follow certain useful routines that govern such things as our nutrition, our hygiene, and our driving (to cite just a few examples). If we choose to stray from these routines, we can suffer unpleasant consequences, from hunger pangs to car crashes.

Since the Church holds us accountable for our commitments, the Church has the duty and the authority to set an objective standard of accountability. Again, this is not unusual. No country lets new citizens write original oaths of fidelity. They're free to write essays or poetry to express their newfound patriotism, but that won't gain them the proper government documents. To become a citizen, they must observe a legal form that is established and commonly recognized.

In matters of importance, proper form is essential and decisive. Marriage is a matter of utmost importance.

❖ ❖ ❖ ❖ ❖

It is important, then, that the couple understand the liturgy and especially their vows. So when I meet with the engaged couple, we walk through the wedding prayers, vows, blessings, and readings, and we discuss their significance.

Ordinarily, the wedding of two Catholics will take place within the context of a nuptial Mass. If the couple includes one Catholic and one Christian who is not Catholic, it may be better to celebrate the Rite of Marriage without a Mass.

Since the non-Catholic spouse cannot receive Holy Communion, a Mass would draw attention to a point of disunity. It could also be awkward for other non-Catholics attending the wedding. (If a Catholic is marrying an unbaptized person, the Church prescribes a special rite for that purpose.)

The nuptial Mass includes most of the parts of the typical Sunday Mass used in a parish. There are the introductory rites; the Gloria ("Glory to God in the Highest"); the readings; the preparation of the gifts and the offertory; the Sanctus ("Holy, Holy, Holy"); the Eucharistic Prayer; the Lord's Prayer and the Lamb of God; the Communion Rite; the dismissal; and the final blessing.

On a typical Sunday, the Church prescribes the readings that will be used. For a wedding, the couple may choose from a list of Scripture readings approved by the Church for use in a nuptial Mass.

There are three readings: the first, from the Old Testament; the second, from one of the New Testament books other than the Gospels; and the third, from one of the Gospels. Between the first and second readings is a responsorial psalm that may be recited or sung.

From the Old Testament, some couples choose the story of God's creation of the first man and woman (Genesis 1 or 2). Others pick one of the Bible's classic love stories, such as the marriage of Isaac and Rebekah (Genesis 24) or Tobiah and Sarah (Tobit 7–8). Still others will select one of the prophetic oracles related to marriage or God's covenant with his people.

The options for the responsorial psalm are equally evocative, expressing gratitude for God's gifts or prayers for domestic happiness and fertility.

For the second reading, the couple may choose from one of the New Testament letters—St. Paul's advice to spouses, for example, or his meditation on marriage as a sacrament of the Church—or from the Book of Revelation's famous passage about the marriage supper of the Lamb of God (19:6-9).

There are many Gospel passages to choose from, such as the wedding feast at Cana, where Jesus performed his first miracle (John 2); Jesus' teachings about marriage (Mark 10 and Matthew 19); Jesus' teaching about happiness in the Beatitudes (Matthew 5); and the commandment to love in Jesus' farewell discourse (John 15).

The readings chosen are significant because they will convey a public message. They will stand as a public statement of what the couple understands about the Sacrament of Matrimony. This will be a teaching moment for everyone attending the wedding. It is certainly a moment of witness to the faith of the bride and groom.

God wants every wedding to be a time of evangelization—a time when people hear the gospel and see it in action. We should hope that the bride and groom are not the only attendees whose lives are changed forever!

❖ ❖ ❖ ❖ ❖

When the time comes for the Rite of Marriage itself, the bride and groom stand before the priest, who addresses them in these words: "My dear friends, you have come together in this church so that the Lord may seal and strengthen your love in the presence of the Church's minister and this community."

We are reminded that this man and this woman are asking the Lord to seal their love publicly, for all the Church to see. The couple declare that they have come freely and without reservation to give themselves to each other and to accept children lovingly from God, if this should be God's plan.

At the heart of the wedding ceremony is the consent of the couple. In fact, of all the seven sacraments, this is the only one conferred *not* by a sacred minister—*not* by a priest, deacon, or bishop—but by the recipients themselves. The priest is present to witness the marriage in the name of the Church and to bless it, but the wedding takes place through the public consent of the couple. It is for this reason that the priest invites the man and woman to declare their consent: "Since it is your intention to enter into marriage, join your right hands, and declare your consent before God and his Church."

The consent of the groom and bride is expressed in the words of a tradition-laden formula. The couple promise "to have and to hold, from this day forward, for better, for worse, for richer, for poorer, in sickness and in health, until death do us part." In another version, the couple each promises to be true to the other "in good times and in bad, in sickness and in health," and ends with "I will love you and honor you all the days of my life."

After receiving their consent, the priest invokes God's blessing on their decision and reminds everyone present that what God has joined, "men must not divide." Everything about the wedding calls attention to its public nature and its permanency.

In another ancient tradition that continues to this day, rings are blessed and exchanged as a sign of the couple's love and fidelity. The ring is worn to announce to all that the two now form one family and are lifelong partners. The rings themselves testify to the permanence of marriage because as circles, they have no end.

What is a part of the human condition from the beginning according to God's creative plan—the coming together in a covenant for lifelong support and procreation of children—has been raised by Christ to the level of a sacrament. The love that brings a couple together becomes a channel of grace. The marriage bond that they form in the exchange of vows becomes an instrument of God's saving action among us.

Thus, marriage—like the priesthood—is viewed by the Church as a sacrament "at the service of communion." Not only do the couple benefit from this sacrament, but so too does the new reality they create—their family. And through their family, the community and the Church will benefit for many years to come.

❖ ❖ ❖ ❖ ❖

In teaching about sacraments, the Church has traditionally spoken about the essential matter, form, and minister.

For the Holy Eucharist, for example, the matter is the bread and wine offered by the Church, the form is the liturgy of the Mass, and the minister is a Catholic priest. For Baptism, the matter is water, the form is the pouring of the water accompanied by certain words invoking the Trinity, and the minister is ordinarily a priest or deacon.

These are vivid signs. They signify great graces given to the Church by almighty God. And they accomplish what they signify. They really convey that grace.

Consider, then, the Church's understanding of marriage as a sacrament. What is the matter of the sacrament? In one sense, it is the bodies of the spouses!

The form? It is the exchange of the vows that signifies the mutual surrender of the spouses' individual lives. What begins with the consent of the vows is eventually consummated, or sealed, in the one-flesh union of the couple.

The ministers of the sacrament, as we have said, are the spouses themselves.

The Church guards the Rite of Marriage because it is a treasured legacy. It is intricate. It is delicate. It is subtle. It is strong. It speaks with a power greater than poetry. It binds with the force of God's law. It is the best possible beginning to the marriage God wants for you.

Bonds of Love

"You're married."

These were the words our celebrant whispered to my husband and me just after we'd exchanged our vows. Surprised—we hadn't thought to ask when in the ceremony we'd be officially wed—Jim and I glowed with joy.

That was less than one year ago. We were twenty-three years old, fresh out of college, and married by our college chaplain in the chapel where we'd met.

Now we live and work in a big metropolitan area, surrounded by neighbors who are also in their twenties. But while marriage might be in their ten-year plans, it falls far below career advancement, self-discovery, and wanderlust. A spouse is someone you find after you've found yourself, as well as paid off those student loans.

And given what secular marriage has become—an accomplishment preceded by financial stability and self-actualization—I can understand why. Fortunately, the Church tells a different story: a story of adventure, of growth, of selfless love. That's why Jim and I got married in the Catholic Church, student loans and all.

It's been both more fulfilling and more difficult than we expected. We've learned that I'm not very nice in the morning, that Jim loses his glasses a lot, and that I forget to replace the toilet paper. That we each have our own insecurities and flaws, and that we're both much more self-ish than we thought. We're working on it.

We've also discovered that I love to cook, that Jim can make me sound like a superhero on my résumé (and that his patience in helping me find a new job knew no bounds), and that being married hasn't shut down our social lives. We've found that praying together is powerful and necessary.

We didn't put off marriage, and I'm glad. Marriage is not meant for perfect people, but we're trying. In the meantime, we're having fun (and even planning a trip to Italy). Above all, we're discovering who we are and how we can grow in love and holiness—a far better path than any ten-year plan!

CHAPTER 9

YOUR LEGACY OF LOVE

I will always remember the excitement in her voice. Not long before, I had officiated at her wedding. And now she was calling to say, "We're going to have a baby!" Her husband added, "Now we are three."

With the arrival of a child comes the thrill of a new beginning—a venture into the unknown. Yet there is also a note of completion. The marriage has accomplished one of its greatest purposes. Something deep in our human nature has been fulfilled. It's striking how often new parents say the same thing: "I didn't know what my life was missing until I held our baby in my arms." People hear that line again and again—and still are surprised when they're feeling the emotion for themselves.

Among the purposes of marriage is the generation and education of children. God, in his plan for human life and love, created us male and female. In this plan, man and woman come together so that in marriage they might express their love and bring forth children, the next generation. The very fragility of an infant and the needs of a child provide the occasion for parents to lavish on them the love, care, nurturing, and education that every human being requires.

We were made to love that way—lavishly. And then children come along requiring that love, needing Mom and Dad for everything. There is no way to love a young child with less than one's whole self because that's what the child needs. God designed children to be needy; their need is nature's most effective way of drawing busy, naturally self-absorbed people outside of themselves.

Children expand the world of their parents. In a sense, they raise their parents. Mom and Dad often arrive at a new stage of maturity unaware because they got there chasing after a toddler.

❖ ❖ ❖ ❖ ❖

"Now we are three."

What a realization! It would not be about *him* any longer. That day had receded far into the past.

Nor was it simply about a starry-eyed couple content in their mutual gaze. Now their lives are directed toward a future that is boundless.

No matter what way God calls us in life, that's the big moment; that's the big discovery we need to make. We need to realize that it's not just about *me* and it's not just about *you*. The sooner we realize that, no matter what our vocation may be, the happier we'll be.

Our lives are directed toward heaven. Children lead us to realize that truth since they force us to think about the distant future. What schools will they attend? What hobbies will they enjoy? What opportunities can we make for them? Whom will they marry?

Gradually, that next generation leads us to recognize that they will likely outlive our own. It is an intimation of mortality yet also a kind of *immortality*. Parents can look at each child and see someone who will take Mom and Dad's traits—their patterns of speech, their life lessons, and their wisdom—into new places and challenging times.

The moral and religious legacy of parents is more important than any other inheritance they might pass on to their children. Money can vanish. So can property. So can heirlooms. But good example endures for ages in those who follow it—and who then inspire others to follow in turn.

Whether or not history remembers a particular married couple by name, each particular couple is making history every day.

❖ ❖ ❖ ❖ ❖

Marriage is a sign of hope. When two become one, it is because they believe that there will be a future worth sharing.

The sign is sealed in a child. A child is like the pledge of a couple's willingness to invest in the future—a pledge of trust in God's providence. Pope Francis said it most eloquently:

Today . . . *children are a sign.* They are a sign of hope, a sign of life, but also a *"diagnostic" sign,* a marker indicating the health of families, society, and the entire world. Wherever children are accepted, loved, cared for, and protected, the family is healthy, society is more healthy, and the world is more human.[12]

The world is healthier when it welcomes children, and I mean that not only in a spiritual sense. Children make grown-ups think long term, sometimes for the first time. I have lost count of the number of parents I've encountered who have quit smoking for the sake of their children, or who have quit drinking, or who have quit working long hours. They'll live longer because they want to see more of the future. They want to live out the classic blessing of biblical religion: "May the LORD bless you . . . ; / may you . . . live to see your children's children" (Psalm 128:5, 6).

So it is that children bring health to the world. And children bring *healing*. They inspire their parents to seek cures that might otherwise be ignored. Children inspire parents to get over vices and addictions. They inspire parents to get over themselves, which is one of the major milestones in anyone's spiritual growth.

We must never forget that there are no perfect couples or perfect families on earth. Everyone is damaged by sin. Everyone is broken. Everyone needs healing.

We are fortunate to live in a time when couples and individuals can benefit from so many advances in medicine, pharmacology, and methods of counseling. Yet even these are more effective when taken up for the sake of love. Love makes every struggle worthwhile.

And make no mistake: every spouse will be called to struggle. During his 1987 visit to our country, St. John Paul II told the American people this:

> *Christian life finds its whole meaning in love, but love does not exist for us without effort, discipline and sacrifice* in every aspect of our life. We are willing to give in proportion as we love, and when love is perfect, the sacrifice is complete. God so loved the world that he gave his only Son, and the Son so loved us that he gave his life for our salvation.[13]

The struggle requires constant *effort*, *discipline*, and *sacrifice*. Yes, marriage is a grace from God. It is a gift, and God is faithful. But God will not force any couple to open their wedding presents, even the gifts that come from heaven.

Husbands and wives must, every day, call upon the grace of the sacrament, never letting their love grow old or cold, even though many decades may have passed since their honeymoon.

❖   ❖   ❖   ❖   ❖

When a husband and wife struggle to live up to their marriage vows, they do more for world peace than a dozen Nobel Prize winners. They do more for the economy than any gathering of the titans of industry. They do more for society than any programs the federal government will ever offer.

If our social order is unraveling today—and many people believe that it is—then it is because individual families are breaking down.

God created marriage to be the one-flesh union of one man and one woman, for life and for the procreation of children. It is astonishing how quickly government and the media have vacated that definition of all its content. It is equally astonishing that so many people have accepted the redefinition, believing they will be happier if they ignore the designs of nature and the revelation of God.

We should not let our hearts be troubled. The gospel was first proclaimed in a world that paid lip service to marriage but didn't live it well. Divorce was common among the ancient Romans, Greeks, and Persians. Jesus noted with sadness that even his own people permitted it.

Yet Jesus himself did not. Nor did his apostles. And his gospel indeed was the force that prevailed.

The ancient world was tired and it was dying. Apart from Christ, it had no hope. The pagan way was one of promiscuity, adultery, easy divorce, abortion, and elected sterility. The pagan world sought to squander everything it had on momentary pleasures that ended in emptiness.

It should not surprise us, then, that Christianity prevailed. It should not surprise us that Christian marriage stood out as a sign pointing the way to an experience of heaven, even here on earth.

The Roman persecutors had to grudgingly admire what they saw in the Church. "See those Christians," they said, "how they love one another." They said that Christians wore love as if it were a brand on their bodies or a tattoo!

Love was what the pagan world was missing. They would never have known, however, if they had not seen it. Those who saw it wanted what they saw. They wanted it for themselves. It made them, one person at a time, seek Christ and find him. And the world underwent its first conversion.

The world wants the same today, but people won't know what they're missing until they see it in Christian homes. They won't know it, perhaps, until they see it in the marriage God wants for you.

Afterword

By Helen Alvaré

I was checking out at a big-box store at the bitter end of a Sunday evening. The young woman ringing up my things, who seemed to be in her late twenties, looked bored and tired. I could see from her bare ring finger that she was unmarried. The nanosecond after bagging my purchases, she returned to reading the celebrity magazine that she had momentarily set aside.

Probably it's just me, a professor of family law, but when I see single young adults in these situations—without interesting work that pays a living wage and without the gift of a spouse and family life—I can't help but take a moment to pray for their future.

The majority of teens and twenty-somethings consistently report that they want to marry and have kids, but today there is a growing chance that less privileged young women and men will not marry at all, or will marry only after having one or two kids. Their odds for temporary cohabition and divorce are also pretty steep. Yet public and private leaders have yet to think seriously about reorganizing economic and social structures and messages to help them.

This young woman could be my daughter. She's somebody's daughter. And she needs help, even in her twenties, because there are some big winds pushing against her: an economy not geared to providing stable work at a living wage for men or for women; a "mating market" where sex is the price of a relationship and marriage isn't on the table even in the face of a pregnancy; a culture treating sex as nothing special, and by turns bemused and aghast that anyone could still believe that sex, marriage, and kids are a logical and desirable package deal.

Likely in the past, Catholic teaching about marriage and family seemed boring and predictable. Law, culture, and religion pretty much agreed that marriage, sex, and the baby carriage were desirable, and in that order. Today, however, there is a vast marriage gap between Catholic teaching and cultural practices, a gap felt most painfully by those with the least education and money. Many only wish they had realistic access to yesteryear's "conventional," enduring marriage followed by parenting! Even more unexpectedly, a confluence of powerful interest groups, academia, the media, and government officials has succeeded beyond anyone's predictions in convincing a near majority that there is nothing special at all about the relationship between men and women. That childbearing and family relationships have no value for society. That marriage is about emotional attachments and sexual intimacy, and nothing more.

The Catholic Church—its pope, its bishops, its lay women and men—wants to help. As Pope Francis told a couple in Naples in early 2015, "How can we go on in a culture that doesn't care about the family? Where marriage is not preferred? I do not have the recipe, the Church understands this and the Lord inspired the convocation of the Synod on the Family. . . . "[14] It is, in fact, an important sign of the times that the Church has devoted so much of its attention to the family during this period of history, precisely when human beings are in need of so much help regarding even quite fundamental truths about marriage and family.

It is also a great relief. The Church's resources are vast and deep. I say this as a professor who has spent decades reading a wide variety of secular and religious materials on the family. Non-Catholics have said the same. At the beginning of the no-fault divorce regime four decades ago, the leading family law authority in the United States, Max Rheinstein, wrote, "The main protagonist for marriage stability has been the Roman Catholic Church. . . . [W]here the faith has been strong, marriage has tended to be stable."[15] He went on to celebrate what he called Catholic teachings' "ideal way of social life": the consultation with priest and family during the engagement, the aversion to adultery, the accepting of setbacks within a broader understanding of the larger meaning of life, the generous acceptance of children, and the respect for authority.

It is in this spirit of the Church's genuine compassion for the human person faced with family troubles, as well as the Church's deep wisdom about things religious, philosophical and practical, that books like this one should be received. As Cardinal Wuerl points out, when it comes to marriage and family wisdom, it's "good to be Catholic!" Max Rheinstein might add, "And it's good to draw wisdom from Catholic tradition even if you're not!"

Like Pope Francis, Cardinal Wuerl recognizes that it's not all hearts and flowers in marriage and family land. There is a sort of silver lining to our troubles, however. The retreat from marriage has made it all the more clear what marriage has been doing all along, and what could be restored if marriage were restored. The decline of marriage is closely associated with crime among fatherless young men, with nonmarital pregnancy, second-generation divorce, educational and emotional setbacks, and so much more. Numerous papers even trace the decline of voting and of women's self-reported happiness to the decline of marriage. Cardinal Wuerl reminds us that St. Augustine taught about marriage from within a similar context of hard-won knowledge: he knew firsthand the sorrows of cohabitation, nonmarital childbearing, and a broken family and, by contrast, the practical and emotional blessings of a Catholic marriage!

Cardinal Wuerl also highlights a few of the things about Catholic marriage that even its ready students may have forgotten. As spouses and parents, we really are supposed to give evidence of what God's love looks like; this will often look like sacrifice and service of a very unglamorous nature. Married couples are also to remind themselves that we don't call marriage a sacrament just to be reverent; marriage "effects" what it symbolizes, and we can actually "lean in" on the graces it offers and ask God for real help when we're struggling.

I often wonder if history will regard the twentieth and twenty-first centuries largely as the era marked by questioning everything about sex, marriage, and family. I guess theoretically human beings could attack even more foundational aspects of the family than they are dispatching today; but it's hard to imagine. When we are questioning whether you are the same sex as your body, whether there is anything important about the union of a man and a woman, and whether we care if children are born, or how or in what circumstances . . . it's hard to imagine what additional aspects of the family we might reject. In these circumstances, it's a great consolation that compassionate and intellectual servant-leaders like Pope Francis and Cardinal Wuerl are taking pains to accompany us.

Helen Alvare is professor of law at George Mason University School of Law. She specializes in family law and the relationship between law and religion. A wife and mother of thirty years, she is also founder of Women Speak for Themselves (womenspeakforthemselves.com) *and a consultor to the Pontifical Council for the Family.*

Endnotes

1. Pope Francis, Address to Participants in the Pilgrimage of Families during the Year of Faith, October 26, 2013.

2. Pope St. John Paul II, Homily at Mass in Uppsala, Sweden, June 9, 1989.

3. See Second Vatican Council, *Dogmatic Constitution on the Church: Lumen Gentium*, n. 40–41.

4. St. Augustine, *Sermons*, 69.2.

5. See, for example, Pope St. John Paul II, Address, October 14, 1993, http://www.vatican.va/latest/documents/escriva_pontefici_en.html.

6. St. John Chrysostom, *On Colossians* 12.5.

7. John Henry Newman, *An Essay on the Development of Christian Doctrine* (London: Longmans, Green, 1909), 40.

8. Pope Francis, Homily at Mass for the Rite of Marriage, St. Peter's Square, September 14, 2014.

9. Pope Francis, Address to Engaged Couples, St. Peter's Square, February 14, 2014.

10. Pope Francis, General Audience, St. Peter's Square, April 2, 2014.

11. St. Augustine, *On the Trinity* 7.34.1.

12. Pope Francis, Homily, Manger Square, Bethlehem, May 25, 2014.

13. Pope St. John Paul II, Address at the Cathedral of Saints Simon and Jude, Phoenix, Arizona, September 14, 1987.

14. Pope Francis, Pastoral Visit to Pompeii and Naples, Meeting with Young People on the Caracciolo Seafront, Naples, March 21, 2015.

15. Max Rheinstein, *Marriage, Stability, Divorce, and the Law* (Chicago University Press), 1972, p. 409.

For Further Reading

Greg and Julie Alexander, *Marriage 911: How God Saved Our Marriage (and Can Save Yours, Too!)* (Ann Arbor, MI: Servant, 2011).

Helen M. Alvaré, *Breaking Through: Catholic Women Speak for Themselves* (Huntington, IN: Our Sunday Visitor, 2012).

Mike Aquilina, *Love in the Little Things: Tales of Family Life* (Ann Arbor, MI: Servant, 2007).

J. Budziszewski, *On the Meaning of Sex* (Wilmington, DE: Intercollegiate Studies Institute, 2012).

Pope Francis, *Family and Life: Pastoral Reflections from His Years as Archbishop of Buenos Aires* (Mahwah, NJ: Paulist Press, 2015).

Pope Francis, *Pope Francis Speaks to Families: Words of Joy and Life* (Frederick, MD: The Word Among Us Press, 2015).

Scott Hahn and Regis J. Flaherty, *Catholic for a Reason IV: Scripture and the Mystery of Marriage and Family Life* (Steubenville, OH: Emmaus Road, 2007).

Francis J. Hoffman, JCD, *Marriage Insurance: Twelve Rules to Live By* (Green Bay, WI: Relevant Radio, 2013).

Richard Hogan, John M. Levoir, *Covenant of Love: Pope John Paul II on Sexuality, Marriage, and Family in the Modern World* (San Francisco: Ignatius Press, 1992).

Pope St. John Paul II: *Familiaris Consortio* (On the Family), Apostolic Exhortation, 1981.

Pope St. John Paul II, *Man and Woman He Created Them: A Theology of the Body* (Boston: Pauline, 2006).

William E. May, Ronald Lawler, OFM Cap, Joseph Boyle, *Catholic Sexual Ethics: A Summary, Explanation, and Defense* (Huntington, IN: Our Sunday Visitor, 2011).

Christopher and Rachel McCluskey, *When Two Become One: Enhancing Sexual Intimacy in Marriage* (Grand Rapids, MI: Revell, 2006).

Brandon McGinley, *The Joys and Challenges of Family Life: Catholic Husbands and Fathers Speak Out* (Huntington, IN: Our Sunday Visitor, 2015).

Pope Blessed Paul VI, *Humanae Vitae* (On Human Life), Encyclical Letter, 1968.

Pontifical Council for the Family, *Love Is Our Mission: The Family Fully Alive* (Huntington, IN: Our Sunday Visitor, 2014).

Gregory Popcak, *For Better . . . Forever!: A Catholic Guide to Lifelong Marriage* (Huntington, IN: Our Sunday Visitor, 1999).

Gregory and Lisa Popcak, *Just Married: The Catholic Guide to Surviving and Thriving in the First Five Years of Marriage* (Notre Dame, IN: Ave Maria Press, 2013).

Gregory Popcak, *When Divorce Is Not an Option: How to Heal Your Marriage and Nurture Lasting Love* (Manchester, NH: Sophia Institute, 2014).

Karol Wojtyla (Pope St. John Paul II), *Love and Responsibility* (Boston, MA: Pauline, 2013).

Katrina Zeno: *Living Together Before Marriage* (West Chester, PA: Ascension, 2009).

 **His Eminence Cardinal Donald Wuerl** is the Archbishop of Washington and was elevated to the College of Cardinals in 2010 by Pope Benedict XVI. Known for his efforts on behalf of Catholic education, he has served as chairman of the United States Conference of Catholic Bishops' Committee on Doctrine, Committee on Education, Committee on Priestly Life and Ministry, and Committee on Priestly Formation, and is a member of the USCCB Committee on Evangelization. He also served as the Relator General for the Vatican Synod of Bishops on the New Evangelization for the Transmission of the Christian Faith. He is the author of numerous articles and books, including *Faith That Transforms Us: Reflections on the Creed* and *The Light Is On for You: The Life-Changing Power of Confession.*

The Cardinal was born in Pittsburgh, Pennsylvania, and received graduate degrees from the Catholic University of America, the Gregorian University while attending the North American College, and a doctorate in theology from the University of Saint Thomas in Rome. He was ordained to the priesthood on December 17, 1966, and was ordained a bishop by Pope John Paul II on January 6, 1986, in St. Peter's Basilica. He served as auxiliary bishop in Seattle until 1987 and then as bishop of Pittsburgh for eighteen years until his appointment to Washington. His titular church in Rome is Saint Peter in Chains.

Also by Cardinal Donald Wuerl

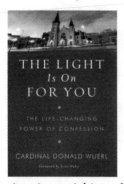

The Light Is On for You
The Life-Changing Power of Confession

Most books about Confession are "how-to" guides. This one goes deeper, showing us how the Sacrament of Reconciliation can heal us and bring us closer to God. Cardinal Donald Wuerl discusses how best to examine our conscience, how to ask the Holy Spirit to reveal our sins to us, and why a regular prayer time is crucial in order to get the most out of Confession and grow in our relationship with the Lord. Scriptural examples as well as stories from the saints and from Catholics today help illustrate his points. This book will change your experience of Confession and brings its fruits into your life!

168 pages, 5¼ x 8, softcover, $12.95 Item# BLITE4

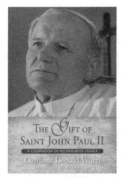

The Gift of Saint John Paul II
A Celebration of His Enduring Legacy

In this book, Cardinal Donald Wuerl, Archbishop of Washington, captures the vision that St. John Paul had for the church and the world. Cardinal Wuerl is known for his gift of teaching the faith, and in this book he explores the spiritual and pastoral wealth of John Paul's writings as found in his encyclicals and apostolic exhortations. The Cardinal unfolds these treasures for us, presenting not only St. John Paul's teachings, but also suggesting how we can apply them in our lives.

288 pages, 6 x 9, softcover, $14.95 Item# BJPGE3

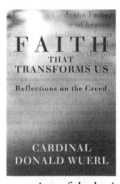

Faith That Transforms Us
Reflections on the Creed

The truths of our faith are more than words—they are living truths that are meant to make a difference in our lives. Every single revelation of God can be life-changing and transforming when we understand it, live it out, and share it with others. This book by Cardinal Donald Wuerl is a positive, uplifting, and joyful presentation of the basic truths of the Catholic faith. With its simple and clear format, it will help Catholics recognize the abundant life awaiting them when they embrace these truths.

Can be used in groups or individually.

152 pages, 5¼ x 8, softcover, $12.95 Item# BAFTE3

theWORD
among us ®
The *Spirit* of Catholic Living

This book was published by The Word Among Us. Since 1981, The Word Among Us has been answering the call of the Second Vatican Council to help Catholic laypeople encounter Christ in the Scriptures.

The name of our company comes from the prologue to the Gospel of John and reflects the vision and purpose of all of our publications: to be an instrument of the Spirit, whose desire is to manifest Jesus' presence in and to the children of God. In this way, we hope to contribute to the Church's ongoing mission of proclaiming the gospel to the world so that all people would know the love and mercy of our Lord and grow ever more deeply in love with him.

Our monthly devotional magazine, *The Word Among Us*, features meditations on the daily and Sunday Mass readings, and currently reaches more than one million Catholics in North America and another half million Catholics in one hundred countries around the world. Our book division, The Word Among Us Press, publishes numerous books, Bible studies, and pamphlets that help Catholics grow in their faith.

To learn more about who we are and what we publish, log on to our website at www.wau.org. There you will find a variety of Catholic resources that will help you grow in your faith.

Embrace His Word, Listen to God . . .

www.wau.org